A Treasury of Sanskrit Poetry

In English Translation

Compiled by

A.N.D. Haksar

INDIAN COUNCIL FOR CULTURAL RELATIONS
NEW DELHI

SHIPRA

2004 Impression
First Published in India in 2002

A Treasury of Sanskrit Poetry

Published by :
SHIPRA PUBLICATIONS
115-A, Vikas Marg, Shakarpur,
Delhi-110092 (India)
Ph : 91-11-22458662, 22500954 Fax : 91-11-22458662
Email : info@shiprapublications.com
www.shiprapublications.com

Laser Typeset by :
Manas Enterprises
Delhi-110032

Printed at :
Chaudhary Offset,
Delhi-110051

P.M.S.

For

Nikhil Narayan Axel Dhruv

and

Freya Nandini Karolina

to remind them of a part

of their cultural heritage

Foreword

With a continuing tradition of at least three millennia, the vast literature of Sanskrit forms an important part of India's cultural heritage. Translations from Sanskrit classics like *Shakuntala* have figured among the earliest publications of the Indian Council for Cultural Relations.

Some years ago the Council brought out *Glimpses of Sanskrit Literature,* a broad informative survey of this magnificent literature by respected scholars, attuned to general interest both in India and abroad. Included in it was a sampling of translations from celebrated Sanskrit works which could give readers a flavour of the language's literary genius.

The appreciative response to that publication, in India as well as outside, encouraged the Council to follow up with the present volume. This is a comprehensive anthology of Ṣanskrit poetry in the best English translation available. The first ever of its kind, it brings together excerpts from a full range of original works translated by a galaxy of distinguished scholars and writers Indian and foreign, including famous names such as Sri Aurobindo and Swami Vivekananda, and Nobel Prize Poets Octavio Paz and William Butler Yeats.

Drawing from sacred and secular, classic and folk literature, this collection features a wide variety of poetry in translation. It has been compiled by former Indian Ambassador A.N.D. Haksar, himself a well known translator from Sanskrit into English, who had also edited the earlier volume for the Council. Expressing deep gratitude for his efforts, the Council has great pleasure in placing its fruit before the public whose comments are welcome as always.

M.K. Lokesh
Acting Director General

Acknowledgements

The compiler and the publisher gratefully acknowledge permission from the following to reprint excerpts from works in copyright:

Sahitya Akademi, New Delhi for excerpts from Chandra Rajan, *The Complete Works of Kalidasa,* Vol. I, and V. Raghavan "Kalividambana", *Indian Literature,* June 1970; Bennet Coleman Co. Ltd., New Delhi and Prof. P. Lal, Kolkata, for P. Lal, "The Messenger", *Femina,* Bombay issue, 8-12 January 1985; Bennet Coleman & Co. Ltd., for excerpts from Pritish Nandy, "Amazing Amaru", 4 October 1990 and "Beguiling Bilhana", 14 November 1990, reproduced by arrangement with *The Illustrated Weekly of India*; Advaita Ashrama, Kolkata, for excerpts from Swami Vivekananda, *In Search of God and Other Poems,* 1977; Mr. J.M. Masson for excerpts from *Sanskrit Love Poetry,* 1977, Columbia University Press, New York copyright © by W.S. Merwin and J.M. Masson; Motilal Banarasidass Publishers, Delhi for excerpts of translations by Barbara Stoler Miller and David Gitomer in Barbara Stoler Miller ed. *Theatre of Memory: The Plays of Kalidasa,* 1999 reprint, first published 1984 by Columbia University Press; Vedanta Press, Hollywood, California, for excerpts from "The Shattering of Illusion", in *Shankara's Crest-Jewel of Discrimination* by Swami Prabhavananda and Christopher Isherwood, 1947; Y.K. Publishers, Agra, for verses from *The Indian Poetic Tradition* by S.H. Vatsyayan, V.N. Misra and Leonard Nathan, 1993; Cassel & Co., London for verses from "Pushan" by Romesh Dutt and "Black Marigolds" by E. Powys Mathers in *An Anthology of World Poetry,* ed. Mark Van Doren, 1929; Chowkhamba Sanskrit Series, Varanasi, for excerpts from *Hymns of the Rig Veda* (1889) tr. R.T.H. Griffith (reprint 1963) and *Hymns of the Samaveda,* tr. R.T.H. Griffith (1893); Mr. Jean Le Mée for excerpts from his *Hymns from the Rig Veda,* Jonathan Cape Ltd., London, 1973; Rupa & Co., New Delhi for excerpts from A.L. Basham, *The Wonder That Was India,* 1959, (Evergreen Encyclopedia, Vol. E-148), Grove Press Inc., New York; Oxford University Press, New Delhi, for permission to reproduce excerpts from *The Thirteen Principal Upanishads,* ed. R.E. Hume, and from Vinay Dharwadkar ed. *The Collected Essays of A.K. Ramanujan* (1999); Motilal Banarsidass, New Delhi, for all of the following: excerpts from *The Buddha Charita or Acts of the Buddha,* ed. E.H. Johnston (Lahore 1936), reprinted 1972, copyright © by Motilal Banarsidass; verses from *Gitagovinda of Jayadeva,* tr. Barbara Stoler Miller, 1984 (copyright © by Columbia University Press, 1977, *Love Songs of the Dark Lord*);

and verses from A.K. Warder, *Indian Kāvya Literature,* Vols. 3, 4, 5 and 6, 1977, 1983, 1992; Penguin Books, UK, for verses from *Poems from the Sanskrit,* (Penguin Classics 1968), tr. John Brough, copyright © John Brough 1988; Penguin Books India Pvt. Ltd., for excerpts from *The Hitopadeśa by Nārāyana,* and *Simhāsana Dvātrimśikā: Thirtytwo Tales of the Throne of Vikramaditya,* both tr. A.N.D. Haksar; The Adyar Library and Research Centre, Chennai, for verse translations from A.K. Warder, *The Science of Criticism in India* (1978); Harper Collins Publishers India Pvt. Ltd., New Delhi, for extracts from A.N.D. Haksar, *Shuka Saptati*, 2000; Sri Aurobindo Ashram Trust, Pondicherry, for passages from the following writings of Sri Aurobindo: *The Translations* and *The Century of Life*, and from *Sri Aurobindo, A Biography and a history,* vol. I, by K.R.S. Iyengar; Jaico Publishing House, Mumbai, for excerpts from Arthur W. Ryder, *Panchatantra*, 1949, (published by arrangement with the University of Chicago Press), originally published in the USA in 1925; Ms. Gwenn A. Miller for excerpts from Barbara Stoler Miller, *The Hermit and the Love Thief*, Columbia University Press, New York (1978); Sri Ramakrishna Math, Chennai, for excerpts from *Bhagavad Gita*, tr. Swami Prabhavananda and Christopher Isherwood; Ms. Nayantara Sahgal, Dehradun, for excerpts from R.S. Pandit, *Ritusamhara,* National Information and Publications Ltd., Mumbai (1947); and Ravi Dayal Publishers, New Delhi, for excerpts from Arvind Krishna Mehrotra, *The Absent Traveller* (1991). Excerpts from "A Tale of Two Gardens", *Collected Poems 1957-1987* by Octavio Paz, translated by Eliot Weinburger, reprinted by permission of New Directions Publishing Corp., copyright © 1986 by Octavio Paz and Eliot Weinburger; lines from "Taittiriya" and "Chandogya" in *The Ten Principal Upanishads* by W.B. Yeats and Shree Purohit Swami, reprinted with the permission of A.P. Wall Ltd., London, on behalf of Michael B. Yeats and Shri Purohit Swami; poem reprinted by permission of the publishers from *Sanskrit Poetry from Vidyakara's 'Treasury'*, ed. and tr. by Daniel H.H. Ingalls, Cambridge, Mass.: the Belknap Press of Harvard University Press, copyright © 1965, 1968 by the President and Fellows of Harvard College, Cambridge, Mass.; poems reprinted by permission of the publisher from *The Saundaryalahri* (Harvard Oriental Series 43), ed. and tr. by W. Norman Brown, copyright © 1958 by the President and Fellows of Harvard College.

Excerpts of translations by Sheldon Pollock are from Sheldon Pollock, "Public Poetry in Sanskrit", in *Glimpses of Sanskrit Literature*, Indian Council for Cultural Relations, New Delhi © 1995 ICCR; translations by George Keyt are from *Gita Govinda* 1947, Kutub Publishers, Mumbai; of Kalidasa by A.W. Ryder are from Arthur W. Ryder, *Kalidasa: Shakuntala and other Writings*, 1912, E.P. Dutton and Co., New York; by Edwin Gerow and Peter Dent from *The Elek Book of Oriental Verse*, 1979, Paul Elek Ltd., London; and by Romesh C. Dutt, from his *The Ramayana and the Mahabharata*, Temple Classics 1899, E.P. Dutton, New York, reprint 1910. Other selections in this book are from *Nalopakhyana*, tr. Sir M. Monier Williams, Oxford University Press, 1879;

Indian Idylls, tr. Sir Edwin Arnold, Trubner and Co., London, 1883; *Song Celestial* tr. Sir Edwin Arnold, *Sacred Writings* Vol. 2, The Harvard Classics (New York, P.F. Collier and Co., 1910); and *Shakuntala* tr. A. Hjalmer Edgren (1894), reproduced in *Six Sanskrit Plays*, ed. Henry W. Wells, Asia Publishing House, 1964. Translations from Bhartrihari by A.N.D. Haksar are reprinted with his copyright permission.

We are grateful to all whose works have been used to compile this book.

Contents

Introduction

This anthology endeavours to bring together a representative selection of Sanskrit verse in the best English translations available. Its objective is to make some of the poetic wealth of the ancient language accessible in this way to a wider circle of modern readers than has been the case so far. It is also intended to provide them a broad perspective of this comparatively less known aspect of Sanskrit literature: not through learned discourse, but by letting the poetry speak for itself. Finally, like any anthology, it is meant primarily for the reading pleasure of those who may peruse its pages.

Translations from Sanskrit into English have a history of over two centuries. The first to be published was that of the *Bhagavadgitā*, by the British East India Company scholar Charles Wilkins, in 1784. The first Indian to translate from Sanskrit into English was Raja Ram Mohan Roy, whose rendition of the *Īśa Upanishad* appeared in 1816. Two early translations deserve note for their subsequent impact. Sir Williams Jones' rendering in 1789 of Kalidasa's famous play *Śākuntala* was among the first works to stimulate Western interest in Sanskrit studies. A major role in setting their direction was later provided by the fifty translated volumes of the *Sacred Books of the East* (1875-1904) edited by Max Müller. Other translations are numerous enough to fill a considerable bibliography; many are of great merit but they have tended to concentrate in particular areas of academic interest.

Modern Sanskrit studies, which gradually took shape from the 19th century onwards, found a special focus in history, linguistics, religion and philosophy. Colonial scholarship sought to learn about India's past through its old language: about the origins and the evolution of the Indic civilization, the development of its institutions and, increasingly, about its religious and philosophical insights. Indian scholars versed in western techniques made their own contribution to the growth of what came to be known as Indology. This discipline paid close attention to Vedic studies and to the later texts of scholarly rather than mainly literary interest. As a result, in contrast to works like the *Upanishads* and the *Bhagavadgitā*, relatively little of the purely poetical literature of Sanskrit has been readily available in English translations. In present popular perception it is best known as the language of religion and philosophy. While its sacred writings also include poetry of high quality, the full beauty of the Sanskrit Muse still remains to be unveiled for other than specialist audiences.

Appropriate translation is the best, if not the only, way of making the poetic riches of any language available to those who do not know it. The qualification has been added to distinguish between literal and literary translation. The first transmits information about ideas and the linguistic form in which they are presented: its main concern is fidelity to the original text, even if the readability of the rendition is thereby impaired. The second needs to convey also the flavour and the feel of the original, apart from being accurate and readable. It must qualify as literature in its own right. Poetry obviously requires translations of the second kind.

Can poetry at all be translated from Sanskrit into as dissimilar a language as English? The trans-cultural difficulties involved are compounded by differences of linguistic construction and literary convention. Earlier scholars like Arthur Berriedale Keith contended that Sanskrit poetry was essentially untranslatable. "English efforts at verse translation," he asserted, "fall invariably below a tolerable mediocrity, their diffuse tepidity contrasting painfully with the brilliant condensation of style, the elegance of metres, and the adaptation of sound to sense of the originals.'[1] While this criticism related mainly to form, the savant Sri Aurobindo struck a similar note with respect to content. "To translate the Veda is to border upon an attempt at the impossible," he observed. "For while a literal English rendering of the hymns of the ancient Illuminates would be a falsification of their sense and spirit, a version which aimed at bringing out all the real thought would be an interpretation rather than a translation."[2]

The comments of Keith and Aurobindo highlight what the American Sanskritist Arthur Ryder described as "the cruel inadequacy of poetical translation."[3] Yet some of Aurobindo's and Ryder's own renderings of Sanskrit verse demonstrate that the obstacles to be overcome are not entirely insuperable. What is important is the end result. A translation of poetry must eventually stand on its own merit to please or move the reader. That several from Sanskrit into English have succeeded in doing so is evident from the testimony of reputable observers.

The Mexican poet and critic Octavio Paz's insightful essay on the beauties of Sanskrit poetry was based in part on his readings of various translations. He wrote that he had "read excellent translations of Kalidasa in English,"[4] and quoted from others of Bilhana's love poems. The British Indologist A.L. Basham listed in his Sanskrit bibliography over a dozen works as "a few only of the best literary translations in English."[5] The Chinese philosopher Lin Yutang wrote about Romesh Dutt's 19th century verse renditions: "My love and true respect for India was born when I first read the Indian epics, the *Ramayana* and the *Mahabharata,* in the present translations" which were "two masterpieces."[6]

A century earlier, the great European poet J.W. von Goethe had expressed fulsome praise for *Śākuntala* on reading it in a German rendition of Sir William Jones' translation. Goethe's well-known epigram remains perhaps the best comment on the translatability or otherwise of Sanskrit poetry:

> If you want the bloom of youth and fruit of later years,
> If you want what enchants, fulfills, and nourishes,
> If you want heaven and earth contained in one name—
> I say *Śakuntalā* and all is spoken.[7]

Good literary translations of the full range of Sanskrit poetry are nevertheless not easy to come by, and more need to be encouraged to make its wealth and variety better known. The present anthology contains excerpts from translations by over forty writers. These include, apart from some distinguished scholars and poets, two winners of the Nobel Prize for Literature and two figures whose national eminence extends beyond their literary accomplishment. If translations by some other writers have not been included, it is either because they were from texts without poetic content; or their source was untraceable; or other translations of the same passage had already been selected. Some translations may have been missed out by inadvertence or due to lack of information which the compiler can only regret.

It is noteworthy that while a few poetical works, for example those of Kalidasa, have been translated by many hands, others have received much less attention, and many have not been translated at all. The last category includes, regrettably, most of the satiric and comic verse in Sanskrit, and much of the epigrammatic poetry collected in anthologies. It may be added that, of the several excellent and still available anthologies of Sanskrit verse compiled between the 10th and the 16th centuries, only one[8] has been fully translated into English so far.

The poetry represented here stretches over a period of about 3000 years or more, depending on the dating of the Vedic texts, which is still uncertain. Including this *śruti* literature and the two famous epics, the translated excerpts in this compilation are drawn from 63 separate works, five Sanskrit and Prakrit verse anthologies[9], and three inscriptions located respectively in India, Indonesia and Nepal. The collection features 59 named poets whose provenance, where known, ranges from Kerala to Kashmir, and from Gujarat to Bengal. Many others are anonymous, while the works of some are known only from anthologies. More recent poetical works from the 17th century onwards, for example those of authors like Venkatādhvarin, Paramānanda and Ghanaśyāma, have gone unrepresented as they are still unavailable in translation.

The selection of excerpts was made on three broad considerations: poetical content; availability of suitable translation; and the need for covering a wide enough time span. Some well know texts were excluded on one of the first two grounds. In considering the suitability of translations where they were available, literal and prose renderings were omitted in favour of those in verse form, except in a few cases which were included mainly to provide representation to otherwise neglected authors.

The reader will find a rich variety of poetry in these translations. They include nature hymns and mystical utterances of profound speculation; epic narratives with evocative descriptions and dialogues; songs and musings; lyrics on many aspects of love; heroic and tragic, erotic and satiric verses; devotional and philosophical poetry; sophisticated compositions from the courts and simple poems of the countryside. The narrative and descriptive verses are presented in longer extracts to convey their sense more fully. A natural counterpoint is provided by the epigrammatic *subhāshita* or "well said" single stanza, which expresses a gamut of compressed emotion or thought, and is a characteristic of classical Sanskrit poetry.

The anthology also includes excerpts from Prakrit and Apabhramśa. While the evolution and chronology of their relationship with Sanskrit continues to be a subject of research, their interconnection is intimate and a part of the same poetic tradition. Sanskrit and Prakrit verses occur frequently in the same works and are quoted in the same classical commentaries on literature. The presence here of Prakrit and Apabhramśa poems in translation is in keeping with this tradition; but each has been identified as such in the table of contents.

To enable them to be seen simply as poetry, the translations are presented here without further comment except some explanatory information in a few cases contained in the endnotes. The order follows generally accepted chronology. The source of the original has been indicated in each case, together with the translator's name. Titles provided by translators for the excerpts have been retained in most cases; where no titles were provided the compiler has devised them, mainly for purpose of reference. Sanskrit verse itself has no tradition for such titles.

Standard practice has been followed in the use of diacritics in transliteration, except in some cases where better known spellings have been preferred or those used by individual translators retained. The letters *ri* and *sh* are used instead of ṛ and ṣ, for example the popular name is written as *Krishna*, which is also common usage, rather than as *Kṛṣṇa*, which is jarring. Similarly *ch* is used instead of c, to write the number five as *pancha*, not *panča*. The letter ṇ is shown simply as *n* where this is the current common usage.

An appendix contains different translations of the same text to give some idea of how they have changed over time. Also included are separate lists giving brief details of the translators, and of the poets who have been translated. Chronological and other details of the latter, it should be noted, are not known with any certainty in most cases.

The compiler would like to thank the Indian Council for Cultural Relations for accepting his proposal for this project, and the Council's Director General and officers for their support and assistance in its implementation, specially in securing permission for use of copyright material. He is grateful to Shri H.K. Kaul and his colleagues at the India International Centre library, and to Smt. M. Vijayalakshmi of the Sahitya Akademi library for their help in his researches; and in particular to Dr. Anthony K. Warder, Professor Emeritus of Sanskrit, University of Toronto, for valuable references from his monumental work *Indian Kāvya Literature*. Above all he thanks his wife Priti for her unfailing support, encouragement, patience and always constructive criticism for which no words can be adequate. The preparation of this anthology has been largely a labour of love for the compiler, and if it can interest readers to explore further the treasure trove of Sanskrit poetry, in translation or the original, that will be his greatest reward.

New Delhi,
Republic Day 2002

A.N.D.H.

THE VEDAS

Rig Veda

1
Ushas: The Dawn

Of all the lights the lightest, this light has come,
This radiance, conceived in a great dazzle of colour,
Rushing ahead of the imminent rise of the sun;
And Night has now given over Her place to the Dawn.

She comes up shining, leading a shining calf.
The Dark One has given over Her mansions to Dawn.
For they are undying kin and follow each other—
Night and the Dawn, exchanging hue for hue.

They are sisters whose endless road is the very same road,
And they take it as surely as if They were guided by Gods;
No clashing there, no halting for Night or Dawn,
Unlike, yet lovely, and in Their thoughts as one.

Her colors flash out as she leads Her exultant dance,
She has opened her gates for us, and opened them wide;
Revealing the world, She shows us how rich we are.
All of the living open their eyes to the Dawn.

Men who were stretched on the ground, She lifts up to act;
Some rise with the golden thought of wealth as an end,
Some, who see little, go on to gape at what's far.
All of the living open their eyes to the Dawn.

You for conquest, and you for a name in this world,
You arisen to find some momentous good,
You moving off toward a different way to live.
All of the living open their eyes to the Dawn.

Child of the kingdom of Light, it's to us She comes;
A faultless girl arrayed in Her lustrous robes,
Lady who oversees our earthly goods,
O Dawn, O lucid Portent, shine on us now. I. 113

V.N. Misra, L. Nathan and S. Vatsyayan

* * * * *

2
Hymn of Creation

Then was not non-existent nor existent: there was no realm of air,
no sky beyond it.
What covered in, and where? and what gave shelter?
Was water there, unfathomed depth of water?

Death was not then, nor was there aught immortal: no sign was there,
the day's and night's divider.
That one thing, breathless, breathed by its own nature:
apart from it was nothing whatsoever.

Darkness there was: at first concealed in darkness,
this All was indiscriminated chaos.
All that existed then was void and formless: by the great power of
warmth was born that unit.

Thereafter rose desire in the beginning, Desire, the primal seed and germ
of spirit.
Sages who searched with their heart's thought discovered the existent's
kinship in the non-existent.

Transversely was their severing line extended: what was above it then,
and what below it?
There were begetters, there were mighty forces, free action here and
energy up yonder.

Who verily knows and who can here declare it, whence it was born and
whence comes this creation?
The gods are later than this world's production. Who knows, then,
whence it first came into being?

He, the first origin of this creation, whether he formed it all or did not
form it,
Whose eye controls this world in highest heaven, he verily knows it, or
perhaps he knows not.

X. 129

R.T.H. Griffith

* * * * *

3
The Wind

O the Wind's chariot, O its power and glory!
  Crashing it goes and hath a voice of thunder.
It makes the regions red and touches heaven,
  and as it moves the dust of earth is scattered.

Along the traces of the Wind they hurry,
  they come to him as dames to an assembly.
Borne on his car with these for his attendants,
  the god speeds forth, the universe's monarch.

Travelling on the paths of air's mid-region,
  no single day doth he take rest or slumber.
Holy and earliest-born, friend of the waters,
  where did he spring and from what region came he?

Germ of the world, the deities' vital spirit,
  this god moves ever as his will inclines him.
His voice is heard, his shape is ever viewless.
  Let us adore this Wind with our oblation. X. 168

R.T.H Griffith

*****

4
Night

The goddess Night has looked abroad
  with her eyes, everywhere drawing near.
    She has put all her glories on.

The immortal goddess now has filled
  wide space, its depths and heights.
    Her radiance drives out the dark.

Approaching, the goddess has expelled
  her sister Dawn.
    Now darkness also disappears.

And so you have drawn near to us,
who at your coming have come home,
as birds to their nest upon the tree.

The clans have now gone home to rest,
home the beasts, and home the birds,
home even the hawks who lust for prey.

Guard us from the she-wolf and the wolf,
and guard us from the thief, O Night,
and so be good for us to pass.

For darkness, blotting out, has come
near me, black and palpable.
O Dawn, dispel it like my debts.

I have offered my hymn as a cow
is offered, Daughter of Heaven. O Night,
accept it, as a victor praise.

X. 127

A.L. Basham

*****

5
The Dawn

Like a youthful maiden, Dawn shines brightly forth,
Stirring to motion every living creature.
Divine Fire was kindled for the use of men;
Dawn created light, driving away the dark.

Sending out her beams, she rose up facing all,
In brilliant robes, resplendent, radiating—
Golden-coloured and glorious to behold,
Mother of plenty, mistress of the days she shone.

Blessed, bearing the sun, the eye of the gods,
Leading her white horse, magnificent to see,
Dawn reveals herself, arrayed in beams of light,
And with boundless glory she transforms the world.

O fair one, banish the enemy with light!
And prepare for us broad pastures free from fear!
Ward off hatred, bring us your priceless treasure!
O bountiful, shower blessings on the singer!

Illumine us with your glorious splendour,
O divine Dawn! Enrich and lengthen our lives,
O Goddess full of grace! Grant us fulfillment
And cows, horses, and chariots in abundance!

O daughter of heaven, Dawn of noble birth,
Whom the men of glory celebrate in hymns,
Establish in us wealth sublime and mighty!
O gods, protect us always with your blessings! VII. 77

Jean Le Mée

* * * * *

6
The Sun

The beams ascend toward the god
Who holds the knowledge of all lives,
So that all things behold the Sun.

Off like thieves, the constellations
Stealthily retreat with the nights
Before the all-beholding Sun.

Now his beams are made apparent
Radiant above the world of men
Blazing and luminous like fires.

Travelling on, in view of all,
Creator of light are you, O Sun,
Shining through all ethereal space.

Now facing all the hosts of gods,
Now facing all men you arise,
Now facing all for all to see.

O Purifier, with your eye
You see life quivering within
The world of creatures, Supreme Lord.

Crossing sky and obscure regions,
You measure out the day with nights,
O Sun, who sees all generations.

Seven mares draw you, O Lord,
In your chariot, Sun Divine,
O Radiant One with hair aflame.

He has yoked the splendid Seven,
The daughters of the Sun's chariot,
And with this willing team, moves on.

Emerging up above the dark,
Toward the higher light we turn;
We have attained the god of gods,
The Sun itself, the highest light.

Rising today, O Love's glory,
Mounting to the highest heaven,
Expel, great Sun, my heart's disease,
And drive the jaundice far away!

To sparrows and to parakeets,
O let us pass my jaundice on!
Likewise unto the yellow birds,
O let us pass my jaundice on.

The Son of the Infinite has
Risen with all his strength and might,
Overcome evil for my sake,
And let me not be overcome! I. 50

Jean Le Mée

*****

7
Indra

Let me proclaim the valiant deeds of Indra,
the first he did, the wielder of the thunder,
when he slew the dragon and let loose the waters,
and pierced the bellies of the mountains.

He slew the dragon lying on the mountain,
for Tvashtri made him a heavenly thunderbolt.
The waters suddenly, like bellowing cattle,
descended and flowed on, down to the ocean.

In his strength he chose the soma—
from three cups he drank the essence.
The Generous seized his thunderbolt,
and smote the firstborn of dragons.

When, Indra, you slew the firstborn of dragons,
and frustrated the arts of the sorcerers,
creating sun and heaven and dawn,
you found no enemy to withstand you.

Indra slew Vritra, and Vyaṃsa, stronger than Vritra,
with his thunderbolt, with his mighty weapon.
Like the branches of a tree felled by the axe
the dragon lay strewn over the earth.

Like an enraged coward he called a challenge
to the great hero, the strong's oppressor, charging.
But he did not escape the force of his blows—
the foe of Indra crushed the clouds together [in falling].

Footless and handless, he still gave Indra battle,
until the thunderbolt struck him hard on his back.
The bullock sought to be match for the bull,
But Vritra, lay, his members scattered afar.

The waters, flowing for man's good, pass over him,
as he lies thus, broken like a reed.

Beneath the waters which he had encompassed
in his great might, Vritra, the serpent lay.

The strength of the mother of Vritra was exhausted,
and Indra bore away her weapon.
The mother lay above, the son below.
Dānu lay like a cow beside her calf.

Fallen in the midst of water-courses,
never pausing, never resting,
floods overwhelm the hidden corpse of Vritra.
In a long darkness lay the foe of Indra.

Lorded by Dāsas and guarded by the dragon
the waters lay, penned in as cows by a Paṇi.
When the opening of the waters was closed up
the slayer of Vritra threw it open.

O Indra, you became a wreath of vapour,
when he impaled you on his lance. Alone
you won the cows, hero, you won the soma,
and you let loose the Seven Streams to flow.

Thunder and lightning availed him nothing,
nor the mist he scattered abroad, nor hail.
When Indra and the dragon fought he conquered,
as he, the Generous, will in future conquer.

And what avenger of the dragon did you see,
Indra, as fear entered your heart when you had killed him,
when you crossed over nine and ninety streams,
as a frightened hawk crosses the skies?

Indra is king of all that moves or rests,
of tame and fierce, the wielder of the thunder.
He is the king of mortals, whom he rules,
encircling them as a wheel's rim the spokes. I. 32

A.L. Basham

*****

8
Aranyāni: Forest Spirit

Lady of the Forest! Lady of the Forest!
who seem to vanish from sight in the distance,
why do you never come to the village?
surely you are not afraid of men!

When the grasshopper replies
to the distant lowing of cattle,
as though to the sound of tinkling bells
the Lady of the Forest makes merry.

Sometimes you catch a glimpse of her, and think it is cattle grazing,
or a house, far away,
and at evening you hear the Lady of the Forest
like the distant sound of moving wagons.

Her voice is as the sound of a man calling his cattle,
or as the crash of a felled tree.
If you stay in the forest in the evening,
you will hear her like a far voice crying.

But the Lady of the Forest will not slay
unless an enemy draws near.
She eats the sweet wild fruits,
and then she rests wherever she will.

Now I have praised the Lady of the Forest,
who is perfumed with balm, and fragrant,
who is well fed, although she tills not,
the mother of all things of the wild.

X. 146

A.L. Basham

* * * * *

9
Pushan

Pushan, God of golden day,
Shorten thou the shepherd's way,
Vanquish every foe and stranger,
Free our path from every danger;
Cloud-born Pushan, ever more,
Lead us as you led before!

Smite the wild wolf, fierce and vile,
Lurking in the dark defile,
Smite the robber and the thief,
Stealing forth to take our life;
Cloud-born Pushan, ever more
Lead us as you led before!

Thou dost pathless forests know,
Thou canst quell the secret foe,
Thou didst lead our fathers right,
Wonder-worker, orb of light;
Grant from thy unfailing store
Wealth and blessing ever more!

Thou hast treasures manifold,
Glittering weapons, arms of gold;
Foremost of the Sons of Light,
Shepherds' god and leader bright,
Grant from thy unfailing store
Wealth and blessings ever more! VI. 54

Romesh Dutt

*****

10
The Gambler

The dangling nuts, born where the wind blows the lofty tree,
delight me with their rolling on the board.
The cheering *vibhīdaka* has brought me joy,
like a draught of soma from Mount Mūjavant.

She did not scold me, or lose her temper.
She was kind to my friends and me.
But because of a throw too high by one
I have rejected my loving wife.

Her mother hates me; my wife repels me—
a man in trouble finds no one to pity him.
They say, 'I've no more use for a gambler
Than for a worn-out horse put up for sale.'

When the conquering die has got his possessions
others embrace the gamester's wife.
His father, his mother, his brothers say of him:
'We don't know him! Take him as a bondman!'

I think to myself: 'I won't go with the others!
I'll stop behind when my friends go to play!'
But then the brown ones raise their voices,
and off I go, like a mistress to her lover.

The gambler goes to the hall of assembly.
'Shall I win?' he wonders. His body trembles.
The dice run counter to his hopes,
and give his opponent the lucky throws.

The dice are armed with hooks and piercing,
they are deceptive, hot and burning.
Like children they give and take again,
they strike back at their conquerors.
They are sweetened with honey through the magic they work on
the gambler.

They play in a troop of three times fifty.
Like the god Savitr, they are true to their laws.
They will not bend to the wrath of the mighty,
and even a king bows low before them.

The dice roll down, the dice leap upwards,
unarmed they withstand the man with arms.
They are heavenly coals, strewn over the board,
and though they are cool they burn up the heart.

The forsaken wife of the gambler sorrows,
and the mother of the son who wanders afar.
In debt, in fear, in need of money,
he goes by night to the house of others.

The gambler grieves when he sees a woman,
another man's wife, in their pleasant home.
In the morning he yokes the chestnut horses
In the evening he falls by the hearth, a beggar.

So to the general of your great army,
to him who is king, the chief of your host,
I say, stretching out to him my ten fingers:
'I risk my all! I am speaking the truth!'

'Don't play with dice, but plough your furrow!
Delight in your property, prize it highly!
Look to your cattle and look to your wife,
You gambler!' Thus noble Savitr tells me.

So make friends with us, be kind to us!
Do not force us with your fierce magic!
May your wrath and hatred now come to rest!
May no man fall into the snares of the brown ones! X. 34

A.L. Basham

*****

11
Thoughts

Our thoughts wander in all directions
And many are the ways of men:
The cartwright hopes for accidents,
The physician for the cripple,
And the priest for a rich patron.
    For the sake of Spirit, O Mind,
    Let go of all these wandering thoughts!

With his dry grass and feather fan
And all his tools of fashioned stone,
The blacksmith seeks day after day
The customer endowed with gold.
    For the sake of Spirit, O Mind,
    Let go of all these wandering thoughts!

I'm a singer, father's a doctor,
Mother grinds flour with a millstone.
Our thoughts all turn upon profit
And cowlike we all plod along.
    For the sake of Spirit, O Mind
    Let go of all these wandering thoughts!

The horse would draw a swift carriage,
The entertainer a good laugh,
The penis seeks a hairy slot
And the frog seeks a stagnant pond.
    For the sake of Spirit, O Mind
    Let go of all these wandering thoughts! IX. 112

Jean Le Mée

*****

Sāma Veda

12
Soma

Hero, the Soma being shed, I pour the juice for thee to drink:
Sate thee and finish thy carouse!
Let not the fools, or those who mock, beguile thee when they seek thine aid:
Love not the enemy of prayer!

Here let them cheer thee well supplied with milk to great munificence:
Drink as the wild bull drinks the lake!
Here is the Soma juice expressed: O Vasu, drink till thou art full:
Undaunted god, we give it to thee!
Washed by the men, pressed out with stones, strained through the filter made of wool,
'Tis like a courser bathed in streams.
This juice have we made sweet for thee like barley, blending it with milk.
Indra, I call thee to our feast.

So, lord of affluent gifts, this juice hath been expressed for thee with strength:
Drink of it, thou who lovest song!
Incline thy body to the juice which suits thy godlike nature well:
Thee, Soma-lover! let it cheer!
O Indra, let it enter both thy flanks, enter thy head with prayer,
With bounty, hero! both thine arms!

Strong, mountain-born, the stalk hath been pressed in the streams for rapturous joy:
Hawk-like he settles in his home.
Fair is the juice beloved of gods, washed in the waters, pressed by men:
The milch-kine sweeten it with milk.
Then, like a steed, have they adorned the inciter for eternal life,
The heath's juice at the festival.

As a good cow to him who milks, we call the doer of good deeds
To our assistance day by day.
Come thou to our libations, drink of Soma, Soma-drinker! Yea,
The rich one's rapture giveth kine.
So may we be acquainted with thine innermost benevolence:
Neglect us not, come hitherward!

Pass by the wrathful offerer; speed the man who pours libations, drink
The juice which he presents to thee!
What is the word addressed to him, god great and excellently wise?
For this is what exalteth him.
His wealth, who hath no store of kine, hath ne'er found recited loud,
Nor song of praises that is sung.
With wealth to our libation come, be not thou angry with us, like
A great man with a youthful bride. II. i. iii, iv and I. iii.

R.T.H. Griffith

*****

Atharva Veda

13
Earth, the Mother

May that Earth, which holds on Her ample lap the ocean,
The rivers, the lakes; which bears the crop-yielding soil,
And is ground for all that breathes and stirs and lives,
May She also bear the fruits of what we have done.

That Earth was born from vast waters, at first was water.
And ancients attended Her growth with their own creations.
Her heart is set on the real, high in the heavens,
And what is undying of Hers is guarded by Truth.

Whatever there is at the core of Your being, whatever
There is in Your air, whatever the power that leaps
From Your length, set us, Mother, among that wealth.
Raise us up. Your are my Mother. I am Your child.

Mother, give me that fragrance You Yourself make,
The perfume that comes from green growing things,
from waters,
The same that heavenly players and dancers desire.
Annoint me with it, so none may wish me hurt.

Your very same fragrance that fills up the lotus pool,
The perfume You had as gift at the marriage arranged
For Dawn by the Gods, the very first perfume of all:
Anoint me with it, so none may wish me hurt.

You who uphold the men who, though mortal,
Are singing and dancing together in exultation,
And uphold the men who, mortal, go out to kill
With furious shouts and the wail of trumpets at war:
O may You, Mother, drive my opponents away,
And make me a man without a rival in all the world.

You Who nurture the five kinds of crops
And are cause for their grains to swell out to ripeness.
O Earth, Wife to the lavish cloud,
It's to You, To Your open hand, that I bow.

Though men cry out in many strange tongues, and profess
A flurry of faiths, You take them all to Yourself.
Give us a thousand streams of Your wealth,
Give, like a cow whose udder is full.

Make us the masters of crowded highways
And of narrower paths, that few, in a hurry, take,
The ways of goodness as well as the ways of evil.
May these be cleared of those who would hurt us or rob us.
And may we receive what is good to receive.

Birds must come swinging round You when they take flight:
The hawk, the swan, and everything that flies,
And the wind that, circling the sky, goes plunging ahead
To drive down the rain, rock the trees, and flare up the fire.
You are the One who issues the wind its force.

Darkness and golden light, the night and day
Were conceived out of You together, O Earth
Wrapped in the circling seasons, wound in time.
Render us good in all our scattered homes. XII. 1

V.N. Misra, L. Nathan and S. Vatsyayan

* * * * *

14
Courage

As the sky even, and even the earth
Do not falter and are not afraid,
So, my life's breath, have no fear.

As the day even, and even the night
Do not falter and are not afraid,
So, my life's breath, have no fear.

As the sun even, and even the moon
Do not falter and are not afraid,
So, my life's breath, have no fear.

As spirit even, and even action
Do not falter and are not afraid,
So, my life's breath, have no fear.

As the truth even, and even chaos
Do not falter and are not afraid,
So, my life's breath, have no fear.

As the past even, and even the future
Do not falter and are not afraid,
So, my life's breath, have no fear. I. 15

V.N. Misra, L. Nathan and S. Vatsyayan

* * * * *

Yajur Veda

15
A Prayer

From the Unreal lead us to the Real.
From darkness lead us unto Light.
From death lead us to Immortality.
Reach us through and through our Self.
And evermore protect us — Oh Thou Terrible!
From ignorance, by thy sweet compassionate Face. XIV. 3 (S.Br.)

Swami Vivekananda

THE UPANISHADS

Kena Upanishad

16
By Whom?

By whom impelled soars forth the mind projected?
By whom enjoined goes forth the earliest breathing?
By whom impelled this speech do people utter?
The eye, the ear—what god, pray, them enjoineth?

That which is the hearing of the ear,
The thought of the mind,
The voice of speech, as also the breathing of the breath,
And the sight of the eye! Past these escaping, the wise,
On departing from this world, become immortal.

There the eye goes not;
Speech goes not, nor the mind.
We know not, we understand not
How one would teach It.

Other, indeed, is It than the known,
And moreover above the unknown.
Thus have we heard of the ancients
Who to us have explained It. I. 1-4

Robert Ernest Hume

*****

Katha Upanishad

17
The One Essential

As the one air, entering into this world,
Becomes the form of what it houses in,
The one Essential, housed in all things born,
Also takes that thing's external form.

As the one sun, the single eye of all,
Is not darkened by flaws in things it sees,
The one Essential, housed in all things born,
And past all grief, is not darkened by grief.

The only Lord, housed in all things born,
He who makes from one a swarm of shapes,
The wise who see Him in themselves, His self,
Their joy is joy that lasts, no other joy.

It is this, the Absolute Joy, they think, and can't be said,
How is it otherwise known, if it shines or does not shine?

In Him no sun, no moon, not one star,
No lighting, how much less these common fires.
But when He blazes up, then all must show;
Then everything flares up immense with him. II. 2.10-15

V.N. Misra, L. Nathan and S. Vatsyayan

* * * * *

Brihadāranyaka Upanishad

18
Tree and Man

As a tree of the forest,
Just so, surely, is man.
His hair are leaves,
His skin the outer bark.

From his skin blood,
Sap from the bark flows forth.
From him when pierced there comes forth
A stream, as from the tree when struck.

His pieces of flesh are under-layers of wood.
The fibre is muscle-like, strong.
The bones are the wood within.
The marrow is made resembling pith.

A tree, when it is felled, grows up
From the root, more new again;
A mortal, when cut down by death—
From what root does he grow up?

Say not 'from semen'
For that is produced from the living,
As the tree, forsooth, springing from seed,
Clearly arises without having died.

If with its roots they should pull up
The tree, it would not come into being again.
A mortal, when cut down by death—
From what root does he grow up? III. 9.28

Robert Ernest Hume

* * * * *

19
The Hymn of Sweetness

The blissful winds are sweet to us.
The seas are showering bliss on us.
May the corn in our fields bring bliss to us.
May the plants and herbs bring bliss to us.
May the cattle give us bliss.
O Father in Heaven be Thou blissful unto us!
The very dust of the earth is full of bliss.
It is all bliss – all bliss – all bliss. VI. 3.6

Swami Vivekananda

* * * * *

Chhāndogya Upanishad

20
You are That

Uddālaka asked his son to fetch a banyan fruit.
'Here it is, Lord!' said Śvetaketu.
'Break it,' said Uddālaka.
'I have broken it, Lord!'
'What do you see there?'
'Little seeds, Lord!'
'Break one of them, my son!'
'It is broken, Lord!'
'What do you see there?'
'Nothing Lord!' said Śvetaketu.
Uddālaka said: 'My son! This great banyan tree
has sprung up from seed so small
that you cannot see it.
Believe in what I say, my son!
That being is the seed; all else
but His expression.
He is truth. He is Self.
Śvetaketu! You are that.' VI.12.1-3

Shree Purohit Swami and W.B. Yeats

*****

Taittirīya Upanishad

21
Learn and Teach

Do your duty; learn and teach.
Speak truth; learn and teach.
Meditate; learn and teach.
Control sense; learn and teach.
Control mind; learn and teach.
Kindle fire; learn and teach.
Feed fire; learn and teach.

Be hospitable; learn and teach.
Be humane; learn and teach.
Serve the family; learn and teach.
Procreate; learn and teach.
Educate your children; learn and teach. I. 9

Shree Purohit Swami and W.B. Yeats

*****

Mundaka Upanishad

22
Two Birds

Two birds, twin images
in plumage,
friends, ever inseperable,
cling to a tree.

One eats the fruit,
eats of the sweet and eats
of the bitter,
while the other watches,
watches without eating.

Buried in the bole
of the self-same tree
one suffers, engulfed
in his impotence.

Yet as he watches the watching
bird, the adorable one, and sees
the sweet bitter glory
as His alone,
He rises, free
from grief. III. 1

A.K. Ramanujan

*****

VYĀSA

Mahābhārata

23
The Humiliation of Draupadi

I

Glassed on Ganga's limpid waters brightly shine Hastina's walls!
Queen Draupadi duly honoured lives within the palace halls,

But as steals a lowly jackal in a lordly lion's den,
Base Duryodhan's humble menial came to proud Draupadi's ken.

"Pardon, Empress," quoth the menial, "royal Pandu's righteous son,
Lost his game and lost his reason, Empress, thou art staked and won,

Prince Duryodhan claims thee, lady, and the victor bids me say,
Thou shalt serve him as his vassal, as his slave in palace stay!"

"Have I heard thee, menial, rightly?" questioned she in anguish keen,
"Doth a crownéd king and husband stake his wife and lose his queen,

Did my noble lord and monarch sense and reason lose at dice,
Other stake he did not wager, wedded wife to sacrifice!"

"Other stakes were duly wagered," so he spake with bitter groan,
"Wealth and empire, every object which Yudhishthir called his own,

Lost himself and all his brothers, bondsmen are those princes brave,
Then he staked his wife and empress, thou art prince Duryodhan's slave!"

Rose the queen in queenly anger, and with woman's pride she spake:
"Hie thee, menial, to thy master, Queen Draupadi's answer take,

If my lord, himself a bondsman, then hath staked his queen and wife,
False the stake, for owns a bondsman neither wealth nor other's life,

Slave can wager wife nor children, and such action is undone,
Take my word to prince Duryodhan, Queen Draupadi is unwon!"

Wrathful was the proud Duryodhan when he heard the answer bold,
To his younger, wild Duhsasan, thus his angry mandate told:

"Little-minded is the menial, and his heart in terror fails,
For the fear of wrathful Bhima, lo! his coward-bosom quails,

Thou Duhsasan, bid the princess as our humble slave appear,
Pandu's sons are humble bondsmen, and thy heart it owns no fear!"

Fierce Duhsasan heard the mandate, blood-shot was his flaming eye,
Forthwith to the inner chambers did with eager footsteps hie,

Proudly sat the fair Draupadi, monarch's daughter, monarch's wife,
Unto her the base Duhsasan spake the message, insult-rife:

"Lotus-eyed Panchala-princess! fairly staked and won at game,
Come and meet thy lord Duryodhan, chase that mantling blush of shame,

Serve us as thy lords and masters, be our beauteous bright-eyed slave,
Come unto the Council Chamber, wait upon the young and brave!"

Proud Draupadi shakes with tremor at Duhsasan's hateful sight,
And she shades her eye and forehead, and her bloodless cheeks are white,

At his words her chaste heart sickens, and with wild averted eye,
Unto rooms where dwelt the women, Queen Draupadi seeks to fly,

Vainly sped the trembling princess in her fear and in her shame,
By her streaming wavy tresses fierce Duhsasan held the dame!

Sacred locks! with holy water dewed at *rajasuya* rite,
And by *mantra* consecrated, fragrant, flowing, raven-bright,

Base Duhsasan by those tresses held the faint and flying queen,
Feared no more the sons of Pandu, nor their vengeance fierce and keen,

Dragged her in her slipping garments by her long and trailing hair,
And like sapling tempest-shaken, wept and shook the trembling fair!

Stooping in her shame and anguish, pale with wrath and woman's fear,
Trembling and in stifled accents, thus she spake with streaming tear:

"Leave me, shameless prince Duhsasan! elders, noble lords are here,
Can a modest wedded woman thus in loose attire appear?"

Vain the words and soft entreaty which the weeping princess made,
Vainly to the gods and mortals she in bitter anguish prayed,

For with cruel words of insult still Duhsasan mocked her woe:
"Loosely clad or void of clothing,—to the council hall you go,

Slave-wench fairly staked and conquered, wait upon thy masters brave,
Live among our household menials, serve us as our willing slave!"

II

Loose-attired, with trailing tresses, came Draupadi weak and faint,
Stood within the Council Chamber, tearful made her piteous plaint:

"Elders ! versed in holy *sastra,* and in every holy rite,
Pardon if Draupadi cometh in this sad unseemly plight,

Stay thy sinful deed, Duhsasan, nameless wrongs and insults spare,
Touch me not with hands uncleanly, sacred is a woman's hair,

Honoured elders, righteous nobles, have on me protection given,
Tremble sinner, seek no mercy from the wrathful gods in heaven!

Here in glory, son of Dharma, sits my noble righteous lord,
Sin nor shame nor human frailty stains Yudhishthir's deed or word,

Silent all? and will no chieftain rise to save a woman's life,
Not a hand or voice is lifted to defend a virtuous wife?

Lost is Kuru's righteous glory, lost is Bharat's ancient name,
Lost is Kshatra's kingly prowess, warlike worth and knightly fame,

Wherefore else do Kuru warriors tamely view this impious scene,
Wherefore gleam not righteous weapons to protect an outraged queen?

Bhishma, hath he lost his virtue, Drona, hath he lost his might,
Hath the monarch of the Kurus ceased to battle for the right,

Wherefore are ye mute and voiceless, councillors of mighty fame,
Vacant eye and palsied right arm watch this deed of Kuru's shame?"

III

Spake Draupadi slender-waisted, and her words were stern and high,
Anger flamed within her bosom and the tear was in her eye,

And her sparkling speaking glances fell on Pandu's sons like fire,
Stirred in them a mighty passion and a thirst for vengeance dire,

Lost their empire wealth and fortune, little recked they for the fall,
But Draupadi's pleading glances like a poniard smote them all!

Darkly frowned the ancient Bhishma, wrathful Drona bit his tongue,
Pale Vidura marked with anger insults on Draupadi flung,

Fulsome word nor foul dishonour could their truthful utterance taint,
And they cursed Duhsasan's action, when they heard Draupadi's plaint.

But brave Karna, though a warrior,—Arjun's deadly foe was he,—
'Gainst the humbled sons of Pandu spake his scorn in scornful glee:

" 'Tis no fault of thine, fair princess, fallen to this servile state,
Wife and son rule not their actions, others rule their hapless fate,

Thy Yudhishthir sold his birthright, sold thee at the impious play,
And the wife falls with the husband, and her duty — to obey!

Live thou in this Kuru household, do the Kuru princes' will,
Serve them as thy lords and masters, with thy beauty please them still,

Fair One! seek another husband who in foolish reckless game
Will not stake a loving woman, will not cast her forth in shame!

For they censure not a woman, when she is a menial slave,
If her woman's fancy wanders to the young and to the brave,

For thy lord is not thy husband, as a slave he hath no wife,
Thou art free with truer lover to enjoy a wedded life,

They whom at the *swayamvara,* thou had'st chose, Panchala's bride,
They have lost thee, sweet Draupadi, lost their empire and their pride!"

Bhima heard, and quick and fiercely heaved his bosom in his shame,
And his red glance fell on Karna like a tongue of withering flame,

Bound by elder's plighted promise Bhima could not smite in ire,
Looked the painted form of Anger flaming with an anguish dire!

"King and elder!" uttered Bhima, and his words were few and brave,
"Vain were wrath and righteous passion in the sold and bounden slave,

Would that son of chariot-driver fling on us this insult keen,
Hadst thou, noble king and elder, staked nor freedom nor our queen?"

Sad Yudhishthir heard in anguish, bent in shame his lowly head,
Proud Duryodhan laughed in triumph, and in scornful accents said:

"Speak Yudhishthir, for thy brothers own their elder's righteous sway,
Speak, for truth in thee abideth, virtue ever marks thy way,

Hast thou lost thy new-built empire and thy brothers proud and brave,
Hast thou lost thy fair Draupadi, is thy wedded wife our slave?"

Lip nor eye did move Yudhishthir, hateful truth might not deny,
Karna laughed, but saintly Bhishma wiped his old and manly eye.

Madness seized the proud Duryodhan, and inflamed by passion base,
Sought the prince to stain Draupadi with a deep and dire disgrace,

On the proud and peerless woman cast his wicked lustful eye,
Sought to hold the high born princess as his slave upon his knee!

Bhima penned his wrath no longer, lightning-like his glance he flung,
And the ancient hall of Kurus with his thunder accents rung:

"May I never reach those mansions where my fathers live on high,
May I never meet ancestors in the bright and happy sky,

If that knee, by which thou sinnest, Bhima breaks not in his ire,
In the battle's red arena with his weapon, dreadful, dire!"

Red fire flamed on Bhima's forehead, sparkled from his angry eye,
As from tough and gnarléd branches fast the crackling red sparks fly!

II. 65-69

Romesh Dutt

*****

24
Death of Abhimanyu

Fatal was the blood-red morning purpling o'er the angry east,
Fatal day for Abhimanyu, bravest warrior and the best,

Countless were the gallant chieftains like the sands beside the sea,
None with braver bosom battled, none with hands more stout and free!

Brief, alas, thy radiant summers, fair Subhadra's gallant boy,
Loved of Matsya's soft-eyed princess and her young heart's pride and joy.

Brief, alas, thy sunlit winters, light of war too early quenched,
Peerless son of peerless Arjun, in the blood of foemen drenched!

Drona on that fatal morning ranged his dreadful battle-line
In a circle darkly spreading where the chiefs with chiefs combine,

And the Pandavs looked despairing on the battle's dread array,
Vainly strove to force a passage, vainly sought their onward way!

Abhimanyu, young and fiery, dashed alone into the war,
Reckless through the shattered forces all resistless drove his car,

Elephants and crashing standards, neighing steeds and warriors slain
Fell before the furious hero as he made a ghastly lane!

Proud Duryodhan rushed to battle, strove to stop the turning tide,
And his stoutest truest warriors fought by proud Duryodhan's side,

Onward still went Abhimanyu, Kurus strove and fought in vain,
Backward reeled and fell Duryodhan and his bravest chiefs were slain!

Next came Salya car-borne monarch 'gainst the young resistless foe,
Urged his fiery battle-coursers, stretched his death-compelling bow,

Onward still went Abhimanyu, Salya strove and fought in vain,
And his warriors took him bleeding from the reddened battle-plain!

Next Duhsasan darkly lowering thundered with his bended bow,
Abhimanyu smiled to see him, kinsman and the dearest foe,

"Art thou he," said Abhima.yu, "known for cruel word and deed,
Impious in thy heart and purpose, base and ruthless in thy greed?

Didst thou with the false Sakuni win a realm by low device,
Win his kingdom from Yudhishthir by ignoble trick of dice,

Didst thou in the council chamber with thy insults foul and keen
By her flowing raven tresses drag Yudhishthir's stainless queen,

Didst thou speak to warlike Bhima as thy serf and bounden slave,
Wrong my father righteous Arjun, peerless prince and warrior brave?

Welcome! I have sought thee often, wished to cross thy tainted path,
Welcome! Dearest of all victims to my nursed and cherished wrath,

Reap the meed of sin and insult, draw on earth thy latest breath,
For I owe to Queen Draupadi, impious prince, thy speedy death!"

Like a snake upon an ant-hill, on Duhsasan's wicked heart
Fell with hissing wrath and fury Abhimanyu's fiery dart,

From the loss of blood Duhsasan fainted on his battle-car,
Kuru chieftains bore him senseless from the blood-stained scene of war!

Next in gleaming arms accoutred came Duryodhan's gallant son,
Proud and warlike as his father, famed for deeds of valour done,

Young in years and rich in valour, for alas! he fought too well,
And before his weeping father proud and gallant Lakshman fell!

Onward still went Abhimanyu midst the dying and the dead,
Shook from rank to rank the Kuru and their shattered army fled,

Then the impious Jayadratha, king of Sindhu's sounding shore,
Came forth in unrighteous concert with six car-borne warriors more,

Darkly closed the fatal circle with the gulfing surge's moan,
Dauntless with the seven chieftains brave Abhimanyu fought alone!

Fell, alas, his peacock standard and his car was broke in twain,
Bow and sabre rent and shattered and his faithful driver slain,

Heedless yet of death and danger, misty with the loss of blood,
Abhimanyu wiped his forehead, gazed where dark his foemen stood!

Then with wild despairing valour, flickering flame of closing life,
Mace in hand the heedless warrior rushed to end the mortal strife,

Rushed upon his startled foemen, Abhimanyu fought and fell,
And his deeds to distant ages bards and wand'ring minstrels tell!

Like a tusker of the forest by surrounding hunters slain,
Like a wood-consuming wildfire quenched upon the distant plain,

Like a mountain-shaking tempest spent in force and hushed and still,
Like the red resplendent day-god setting on the western hill,

Like the moon serene and beauteous quenched in eclipse dark and pale,
Lifeless slumbered Abhimanyu when the softened starlight fell!

Done the day of death and slaughter, darkening shadows close around,
Wearied warriors seek for shelter on the vast and tented ground,

Soldiers' camp-fires brightly blazing, tent-lights shining from afar,
Cast their fitful gleam and radiance on the carnage of the war!

VII (abridged)

Romesh Dutt

* * * * *

25
Oblation to Karna

Sacred Ganga, ample-bosomed, sweeps along in regal pride,
Rolling down her limpid waters through high banks on either side,

Childless dames and weeping widows thither in their anguish came,
Due and holy rites to render to departed chiefs of fame.

Casting forth their jewelled girdles, gems and scarfs belaced with gold,
Gave oblations of the water unto warriors true and bold,

Unto fathers, unto husbands, unto sons in battle slayed,
Offerings of the sacred water sorrowing wives and mothers made.

And so great the host of mourners wending to perform the rite,
That their footsteps made a pathway in the sad and sacred site,

And the shelving banks of Ganga peopled by the sorrowing train,
Wide-expanding, vast and sealike, formed a scene of woe and pain!

But a wave of keener sorrow swept o'er Pritha's heaving breast,
As unto her weeping children thus her secret she expressed:

"*He, my sons, the peerless bowman, mighty in his battle-car,*
Who by will of fate untimely was by Arjun slain in war,

He whom as the son of Radha, chariot-driver ye bave thought,
But who shone with Surya's lustre as his countless foes be fought,

He who faced your stoutest warriors and in battle never failed,
Bravely led the Kuru forces and in danger never quailed,

He who knew no peer in prowess, owned in war no haughtier name,
Yielded life but not his honour and by death hath conquered fame,

He in truth who never faltered, never left his vow undone,
Offer unto him oblation, Karna was my eldest son!

Karna was your honoured elder and the Sun inspired his birth,
Karna in his rings and armour Sun-like trod the spacious earth!"

Pritha spake; the Pandav brothers groaned in penitence and pain,
And they wept in woe and anguish for the brother they had slain,

Hissing forth his sigh of anguish like a crushed and wounded snake
Sad Yudhishthir to his mother thus his inward feelings spake:

"Didst thou, mother, bear the hero fathomless like ocean dread,
Whose unfailing glistening arrows like its countless billows sped,

Didst thou bear that peerless archer all-resistless in his car,
Sweeping with the roar of ocean through the shattered ranks of war?

Didst thou hide the mighty warrior, mortal man of heavenly birth,
Crushing 'neath his arm of valour all his foemen on the earth,

Didst thou hide the birth and lineage of that chief of deathful ire,
As a man in folds of garments seeks to hide the flaming fire?

Arjun wielder of *Gandiva* was for us no truer stay
Than was Karna for the Kurus in the battle's dread array,

Monarchs matched not Karna's glory nor his deeds of valour done,
Midst the mighty car-borne warriors mightiest warrior Karna shone!

Woe to us! our eldest brother we have in the battle slain,
And our nearest dearest elder fell upon the gory plain,

Not the death of Abhimanyu from the fair Subhadra torn,
Not the slaughter of the princes by the proud Draupadi borne,

Not the fall of friends and kinsmen and Panchala's mighty host,
Like thy death afflicts my bosom, noble Karna loved and lost!

Monarch's empire, victor's glory, all the treasures earth can yield,
Righteous bliss and heavenly gladness, harvest of the heavenly field,

All that wish can shape and utter, all that nourish hope and pride,
All were ours, O noble Karna, hadst thou rested by our side,

And this carnage of the Kurus these sad eyes had never seen,
Peace had graced our blessed empire, happy would the earth have been!"

Long bewailed the sad Yudhishthir for his elder loved and dead,
And oblation of the water to the noble Karna made,

And the royal dames of Kuru viewed the sight with freshening pain,
Wept to see the good Yudhishthir offering to his brother slain,

And the widowed queen of Karna with the women of his house
Gave oblations to her hero, wept her loved and slaughtered spouse!

Done the rites to the departed, done oblations to the dead,
Slowly then the sad survivors on the river's margin spread,

Far along the shore and sandbank of the sacred sealike stream
Maid and matron lave their bodies 'neath the morning's holy beam,

And ablutions done, the Kurus slow and sad and cheerless part,
Wend their way to far Hastina with a void and vacant heart. XI. 27

Romesh Dutt

* * * * *

26
The Mother to Her Son

Out, arise, thou coward! lie not thus upon the ground o'erthrown
Shorn of pride, thy foes' delight, thy friends' shame, making fruitless moan.
Easily a paltry river with the meagre floods o'erflows,
Easily the fieldmouse with her mite of grain contented goes,
Easily the coward ceases, fainting from his great emprise.
Break the serpent's fangs between thy hands and perish, not as dies
Impotent a whining dog, go deathward, but as circles o'er his pray,
But as wheels an angry falcon through the wide and azure day
Watching for his moment, thou in fearless silence wait thy time
Or with resonant and far-voiced challenge waken war sublime.
Wherefore like a dead thing thunder-blasted liest thou on the ground?
Rise, thou coward, seek not slumber while the victors jeer around.
Turn not miserably to thy set, but smiting with the sword
Make the world re-eho! deem that thou wast born to be its lord,
Not with middle place content nor abject; all subjection spurn.
Stand erect, whate'er befall thee, roaring on thy hunters turn.
Blaze out like a firebrand even if for a moment burning high,
Not like the poor fire of husks that smoulders long, afraid to die.
Better is the swift and glorious flame that mounting dies of power,
Not to smoke in squalid blackness, hour on wretched futile hour.
Out to battle, do thy man's work, falter not in high attempt;
So a man is quit before his God and saved from self-contempt.
For the great heart grieves not though he lose the glorious crown of strife,
But he does the work before him, holding cheap his body's life.
Show thy prowess, he the hero thou wast born, with flashing glaive,
Hew thy way with God before thee to the heaven of the brave. V. 131

Sri Aurobindo

27
The Bridal of Damayanti

Came the day of happy omen, moonday meet, and moment apt;
Bhima to the Svayaṃvara summoned all the lords of earth.
One and all, upon the instant, rose th' enamoured lords of earth,
Suitors all to Damayanti in their loving haste they came.
They, the court with golden columns rich, and glittering portal arch,
Like the lions on the mountains entered they the hall of state.
There the lords of earth were seated, each upon his several throne;
All their fragrant garlands wearing, all with pendant ear-gems rich.
Arms were seen robust and vigorous as the ponderous battle mace,
Some like the five-headed serpents, delicate in shape and hue:
With bright locks profuse and flowing, fine-formed nose, and eye and brow,
Shone the faces of the Rajas like the radiant stars in heaven.
As with serpents, Bhogavati, the wide hall was full of kings;
As the mountain-caves with tigers, with the tiger-warriors full.
Damayanti in her beauty entered on that stately scene,
With her dazzling light entrancing every eye and every soul.
O'er her lovely person gliding all the eyes of those proud kings;
There were fixed, there moveless rested, as they gazed upon the maid.
Then as they proclaimed the Rajas, (by his name was each proclaimed,)
In dismay saw Bhima's daughter, five in garb, in form the same.
On those forms, all undistinguished each from each, she stood and gazed.
In her doubt Vidarbha's princess Nala's form might not discern,
Whichsoe'er the form she gazed on, him her Nala, him she thought.
She within her secret spirit deeply pondering, stood and thought:
'How shall I the gods distinguish? royal Nala how discern?'
Pondering thus Vidarbha's maiden in the anguish of her heart—
Th' attributes of the immortals sought, as heard of yore, to see.
'Th' attributes of each celestial, that our aged sires describe,
As on earth they stand before me, not of one may I discern.'
Long she pondered in her silence, and again, again she thought.
To the gods, her only refuge, turned she at this trying hour.
With her voice and with her spirit she her humble homage paid.
Folding both her hands and trembling to the gods the maiden spake:
'As when heard the swan's sweet language chose I then Nishadha's king,
By this truth I here adjure ye, oh, ye gods, reveal my lord!
As in word or thought I swerve not from my faith, all-knowing powers!
By this truth I here adjure ye, oh, ye gods, reveal my lord!

As in word or thought I swerve not from my faith, all-knowing powers!
By this truth I here adjure ye, oh, ye gods, reveal my lord!
As the gods themselves have destined for my lord Nishadha's king;
By this truth I here adjure ye, oh, ye gods, my lord reveal!
As my vow, so pledged to Nala, holily must be maintained,
By this truth I here adjure ye, oh, ye gods my lord reveal!
Each the form divine assume ye, earth's protectors, mighty lords;
So shall I discern my Nala, I shall know the king of men.'
As they heard sad Damayanti uttering thus her piteous prayer,
At her high resolve they wonder, steadfast truth and fervent love,
Holiness of soul, and wisdom, to her lord her constant faith.
As she prayed, the gods obedient stood with attributes revealed:
With unmoistened skins the Immortals saw she, and with moveless eyes;
Fresh their dust-unsullied garlands hovered they, nor touched the earth.
By his shadow doubled, dust-soiled, garlands-drooping, moist with sweat,
On the earth Nishadha's monarch stood confessed, with twinkling eyes:
On the gods an instant gazed she, then upon the king of men;
And of right king Bhima's daughter named Nishadha's king her lord.
Modestly the large-eyed maiden lifted up his garment's hem,
Round his shoulders threw she lightly the bright zone of radiant flowers.
So she chose him for her husband, Nala, that high-hearted maid.
Then 'alas! alas!' burst wildly, from that conclave of the kings,
And 'well done, well done,' as loudly, from the gods and sages broke.
All in their ecstatic wonder glorified Nishadha's king.
Then to royal Damayanti, Virasena's kingly son,
To that slender-waisted damsel spake he comfort in his joy;
'Since thou'st own'd me for thine husband, in the presence of the gods,
For thy faithful consort know me, aye delighting in thy words.
While this spirit fills this body, maiden with the smile serene!
Thine am I, so long thine only, this the solemn truth I vow.'
Thus he gladdened Damayanti with the assurance of his faith.
Then, rejoicing in each other, that blest pair, upon the gods
Led by Agni, gazed in homage, on their great protectors gazed. III. 6.53

Sir M. Monier Williams

* * * * *

28
Savitri and the God of Death

Then, having reached where woodland fruits did grow,
They gathered those, and filled a basket full;
And afterwards the Prince plied hard his axe,
Cutting the sacred fuel. Presently
There crept a pang upon him; a fierce throe
Burned through his brows, and, all asweat, he came
Feebly to Savitri, and moaned: 'O wife,
I am thus suddenly too weak for work;
My veins throb, Savitri; my blood runs fire;
It is as if a threefold fork were plunged
Into my brain. Let me lie down, fair Love!
Indeed, I cannot stand upon my feet.'

Thereon that noble lady, hastening near,
Stayed him, that would have fallen, with quick arms;
And, sitting on the earth, laid her lord's head
Tenderly in her lap. So bent she, mute,
Fanning his face, and thinking 'twas the day—
The hour—which Narada named—the sure fixed date
Of dreadful end—when, lo! before her rose
A shade majestic. Rcd his garments were,
His body vast and dark, like fiery suns
The eyes which burned beneath his forehead-cloth;
Armed was he with a noose, awful of mien
This Form tremendous stood by Satyavan,
Fixing its gaze upon him. At the sight
The fearful Princess started to her feet.
Heedfully laying on the grass his head,
Up started she, with beating heart, and joined
Her palms for supplication, and spake thus
In accents tremulous: 'Thou seem'st some god;
Thy mien is more than mortal; make me know
What god thou art, and what thy purpose here.'

And Yama (the dreadful God of death) said;
'Thou art a faithful wife, O Savitri,
True to thy vows, pious, and dutiful;

Therefore I answer thee. Yama I am!
This Prince, thy lord, lieth at point to die;
Him will I straightway bind and bear from life;
This is my office, and for this I come.'
Then Savitri spake sadly: 'It is taught,
Thy messengers are sent to fetch the dying;
Why is it, Mightiest, thou art come thyself?'

In pity of her love, the Pitiless
Answered,—the King of all the Dead replied:
'This was a Prince unparalleled, thy lord;
Virtuous as fair, a sea of goodly gifts,
Not to be summoned by a meaner voice
Than Yama's own: therefore is Yama come.'

With that the gloomy God fitted his noose,
And forced forth from the Prince the soul of him—
Subtile, a thumb in length—which being reft,
Breath stayed, blood stopped, his body's grace was gone,
And all life's warmth to stony coldness turned.
Then, binding it, the Silent Presence bore
Satyavan's soul away toward the South.

But Savitri the Princess followed him:
Being so bold in wifely purity,
So holy by her love: and so upheld,
She followed him.

Presently Yama turned.
'Go back,' quoth he; 'pay him the funeral dues.
Enough, O Savitri! is wrought for love;
Go back! too far already hast thou come.'
Then Savitri made answer: 'I must go
Where my lord goes, or where my lord is borne;
Nought other is my duty. Nay, I think,
By reason of my vows, my services
Done to the Gurus, and my faultless love,
Grant but thy grace, I shall unhindered go.
The sages teach that to walk seven steps,
One with another, maketh good men friends;
Beseech thee, let me say a verse to thee:—

Be master of thyself, if thou wilt be
Servant of Duty. Such as thou shalt see
Not self-subduing, do no deeds of good
In youth or age, in household or in wood.
But wise men know that virtue is best bliss,
And all by some one way may reach to this.
It needs not men should pass through orders four
To come to knowledge: doing right is more
Than any learning; therefore sages say
Best and most excellent is Virtue's way.'

Spake Yama then: 'Return! yet I am moved
By those soft words; justly their accents fell,
And sweet and reasonable was their sense.
See, now, thou faultless one. Excepts this life
I bear away, ask any boon from me;
It shall not be denied.'

Savitri said:
'Let, then, the King, my husband's father, have
His eyesight back, and be his strength restored,
And let him live anew, strong as the sun.'

'I give this gift,' Yama replied: 'thy wish,
Blameless, shall be fulfilled. But now go back;
Already art thou wearied, and our road
Is hard and long. Turn back, lest thou, too, die.'

The Princess answered: 'Weary am I not,
So I walk nigh my lord. Where he is borne,
Thither wend I. Most mighty of the gods,
I follow whereso'er thou takest him.
A verse is writ on this, if thou wouldst hear:

There is nought better than to be
With noble souls in company:
There is nought dearer than to wend
With good friends faithful to the end.
This is the love whose fruit is sweet;
Therefore to bide therein is meet.'

Spake Yama, smiling: 'Beautiful! Thy words
Delight me; they are excellent, and teach
Wisdom unto the wise, singing soft truth.
Look, now! Except the life of Satyavan,
Ask yet another—any—boon from me.'

Savitri said: 'Let then, the pious King,
My husband's father, who hath lost his throne,
Have back the Raj; and let him rule his realm
In happy righteousness. This boon I ask.'

'He shall have back the throne,' Yama replied,
'And he shall reign in righteousness: these things
Will surely fall. But thou, gaining thy wish,
Return anon; so shalt thou 'scape sore ill.'

'Ah, awful God! Who hold'st the world in leash,'
The Princess said, 'restraining evil men,
And leading good men,—even unconscious,—there
Where they attain, hear yet these famous words:

The constant virtues of the good are tenderness and love
To all that lives—in earth, air, sea—great, small—below, above,
Compassionate of heart, they keep a gentle thought for each,
Kind in their actions, mild in will, and pitiful of speech;
Who pitieth not he hath not faith; full many an one so lives,
But when an enemy seeks help the good man gladly gives.'

'As water to the thirsting,' Yama said,
'Princess, thy words melodious are to me.
Except the life of Satyavan thy lord,
Ask one boon yet again, for I will grant.'
Answer made Savitri: 'The King, my sire,
Hath no male child. Let him see many sons
Begotten of his body. Who may keep
The royal line long regnant. This I ask.'

'So it shall be!' the Lord of death replied;
'A hundred fair preservers of his race
Thy sire shall boast. But this wish being won,
Return, dear Princess; thou hast come too far.'

'It is not far for me,' quoth Savitri,
'Since I am near my husband; nay, my heart
Is set to go as far as to the end;
But hear these other verses, if thou wilt:

By that sunlit name thou bearest,
Thou, Vaivaswata! art dearest;
Those that as their Lord proclaim thee,
King of Righteousness do name thee;
Better than themselves the wise
Trust the righteous. Each relies
Most upon the good, and makes
Friendship with them. Friendship takes
Fear from hearts; yet friends betray,
In good men we may trust alway.'

'Sweet lady ,' Yama said, 'never were words
Spoke better; never truer heard by ear;
Lo! I am pleased with thee. Except this soul,
Ask one gift yet again, and get thee home.'

'I ask thee, then,' quickly the Princess cried,
'Sons, many sons, born of my body: boys;
Satyavan's children; lovely, valiant, strong.
Continuers of their line. Grant this, kind god'

'I grant it,' Yama answered; 'thou shalt bear
Those sons thy heart desireth, valiant, strong.
Therefore go back, that years be given thee.
Too long a path thou treadest, dark and rough.'
But, sweeter than before, the princess sang:

'In paths of peace and virtue
Always the good remain;
And sorrow shall not stay with them,
Nor long access of pain;
At meeting or at parting
Joys to their bosom strike;
For good to good is friendly,
And virtue loves her like.
The great sun goes his journey

By their strong truth impelled;
By their pure lives and penances
Is earth itself upheld;
Of all which live or shall live
Upon its hills and fields,
Pure hearts are the "protectors",
For virtue saves and shields.

'Never are noble spirits
Poor while their like survive;
True love has gems to render,
And virtue wealth to give.
Never is lost or wasted
The goodness of the good;
Never against a mercy,
Against a right, it stood;
And seeing this, that virtue
Is always friend to all,
The virtuous and true-hearted,
Men their "protectors" call.'

'Line for line, Princess! as thou sangest so,'
Quoth Yama, 'all that lovely praise of good,
Grateful to hallowed minds, lofty in sound,
And couched in dulcet numbers—word by word—
Dearer thou grew'st to me. O thou great heart,
Perfect and firm! ask any boon from me,—
Ask an incomparable boon!"

She cried
Swiftly, no longer stayed: 'Not heaven I crave,
Nor heavenly joys, nor bliss incomparable,
Hard to be granted even by thee; but *him*,
My sweet lord's life, without which I am dead;
Give me that gift of gifts! I will not take
Aught less without him,—not one boon,—no praise,
No splendours, no reward,- not even those sons
Whom thou didst promise. Ah, thou wilt not, now,
Bear hence the father of them, and my hope!
Make thy free word good; give me Satyavan
Alive once more.'

And thereupon the God—
The Lord of Justice, high Vaivaswata—
Loosened the noose and freed the Prince's soul,
And gave it to the lady, saying this,
With eyes grown tender: 'See, thou sweetest queen
Of women, brightest jewel of thy kind!
Here is thy husband. He shall live and reign
Side by side with thee,—saved by thee,—in peace,
And fame, and wealth, and health, many long years;
For pious sacrifices world-renowned.
Boys shalt thou bear to him, as I did grant,—
Kshatriya kings, fathers of kings to be,
Sustainers of thy sire. Also, thy sire
Shall see his name upheld by sons of sons,
Like the immortals, valiant, Malavas.' II. 291-7, III. 281

Sir Edwin Arnold

❄ ❄ ❄ ❄ ❄

Bhagavadgītā

29
The Sorrow of Arjuna

Krishna, Krishna,
Now as I look on
These my kinsmen
Arrayed for battle,
My limbs are weakened,
My mouth is parching,
My body trembles,
My hair stands upright,
My skin seems burning,
The bow Gandiva
Slips form my hand,
My brain is whirling
Round and round,
I can stand no longer:
Krishna, I see such

Omens of evil!
What can we hope from
This killing of kinsmen?
What do I want with
Victory, empire,
Or their enjoyment?
O Govinda,
How can I care for
Power or pleasure,
My own life, even,
When all these others,
Teachers, fathers,
Grandfathers, uncles,
Sons and brothers,
Husbands of sisters,
Grandsons and cousins,
For whose sake only
I could enjoy them
Stand here ready
To risk blood and wealth
In war against us?
Knower of all things,
Though they should slay me
How could I harm them?
I cannot wish it:
Never, never,
Not though it won me
The throne of the three worlds;
How much the less for
Earthly lordship! I. 28-34

Swami Prabhavananda and Christopher Isherwood

*****

30
The Vision

Then, O king! the God, so saying,
Stood, to Prithā's Son displaying
All the splendour, wonder, dread
Of His vast Almighty-head.
Out of countless eyes beholding,
Out of countless mouths commanding,
Countless mystic forms enfolding
In one Form: supremely standing
Countless radiant glories wearing,
Countless heavenly weapons bearing,
Crowned with garlands of star-clusters,
Robed in garb of woven lustres,
Breathing from His perfect Presence
Breaths of all delicious essence
Of all sweetest odors; shedding
Blinding brilliance, overspreading—
Boundless, beautiful—all spaces
From His all-regarding faces;
So He showed! If there should rise
Suddenly within the skies
Sunburst of a thousand suns
Flooding earth with rays undeemed of,
Then might be that Holy One's
Majesty and glory dreamed of. XI. 9-12

Sir Edwin Arnold

* * * * *

VĀLMĪKI

Rāmāyaṇa

31
Rama and Sita

But Sita all the while, unhappy child,
Worshipped propitious gods. Her mind in dreams
August and splendid coronations dwelt
And knew not of that woe. Royal she worshipped,
A princess in her mind and mood, and sat
With expectation thrilled. To whom there came
Rama, downcast and sad, his forehead moist
From inner anguish. Dark with thought and shaken
He entered his august and jubilant halls.
She started from her seat, transfixed, and trembled,
For all the beauty of his face was marred,
Who when he saw his young beloved wife
Endured no longer; all his inner passion
Of tortured pride was opened in his face.
And Sita, shaken, cried aloud, "What grief
Comes in these eyes? Was not today thine hour
When Jupiter, the imperial planet, joins
With Pushya, that high constellation? Why
Art thou then pale, disturbed? Where is thy pomp,
Thy crowning where? No foam-white softness silk
With hundred-shafted canopy o'erhues
Thy kingly head, no fans o'erwave thy face
Like birds that beat their bright wings near a flower;
Minstrel nor orator attends thy steps
To hymn thy greatness, nor are heralds heard
Voicing high stanzas. Who has then forbade
The honeyed curds that Brahmins Veda-wise
Should pour on thy anointed brow, — the throngs
That should behind thee in a glory surge,—
The ministers and leading citizens
And peers and commons of the provinces
And commons metropolitan? Where stays
Thy chariot by four gold-clad horses drawn,

Trampling, magnificent, wide-maned? thy huge
High-omened elephant, a thunder-cloud
Or moving mountain in thy front? thy seat
Enriched with curious gold? Such are the high
Symbols men lead before anointed kings
Through streets flower-crowned. But thou com'st careless, dumb,
Alone. Or if thy coronation still,
Hero, prepares and nations for thee wait,
Wherefore comes this grey face not seen before
In which there is no joy?" Trembling she hushed.
Then answered her the hope of Raghou's line:
"Sita, my sire exiles me to the woods.
O high-born soul, O firm religious mind,
Be strong and hear me. Dussaruth my sire,
Whose royal word stands as the mountains pledged
To Bharath's mother boons of old, her choice
In her selected time, who now prefers
Athwart the coronation's sacred pomp
Her just demand; me to the Dundac woods
For fourteen years exiled and in my stead
Bharath, my brother, royally elect
To this wide empire. Therefore I come, to visit
And clasp thee once, ere to far woods I go.
But thou before King Bharath speak my name
Seldom; thou knowcst great and wealthy men
Are jealous and endure not others' praise.
Speak low and humbly of me when thou speakest,
Observing all his moods; for only thus
Shall man survive against a monarch's brow.
He is a king, therefore to be observed;
Holy, since by a monarch's sacred hands
Anointed to inviolable rule.
Be patient; thou art wise and good. For I
Today begin exile, Sita, today
Leave thee, O Sita. But when I am gone
Into the paths of the ascetics old
Do thou in vows and fasts spend blamelessly
Thy lonely seasons. With the dawn arise
And when thou hast adored the Gods, bow down
Before King Dussaruth, my father, then
Like a dear daughter tend religiously

Cowshalya, my afflicted mother old;
Nor her alone, but all my father's queens
Gratify with sweet love, smiles, blandishments
And filial claspings; — they my mothers are,
Nor than the breasts that suckled me less dear.
But mostly I would have thee show, beloved,
To Shatrughna and Bharath, my dear brothers,
More than my life-blood dear, a sister's love
And a maternal kindness. Cross not Bharath
Even slightly in his will. He is thy king,
Monarch of thee and monarch of our house
And all this nation. 'Tis by modest awe
And soft obedience and high toilsome service
That princes are appeased, but being crossed
Most dangerous grow the wrathful hearts of kings
And mischiefs mean. Monarchs incensed reject
The sons of their own loins who durst oppose
Their mighty policies, and raise, of birth
Though vile, the strong and serviceable man.
Here then obedient dwell unto the King,
Sita; but I into the woods depart." II. 26

Sri Aurobindo

*****

32
Sita's Vow

Rama spake, and soft-eyed Sita, ever sweet in speech and word,
Stirred by loving woman's passion boldly answered thus her lord:

"Do I hear my husband rightly, are these words by Rama spake,
And her banished lord and husband will the wedded wife forsake?

Lightly I dismiss the counsel which my lord hath lightly said,
For it ill beseems a warrior and my husband's princely grade!

For the faithful woman follows where her wedded lord may lead,
In the banishment of Rama, Sita's exile is decreed,

Sire nor son nor loving brother rules the wedded woman's state,
With her lord she falls or rises, with her consort courts her fate,

If the righteous son of Raghu wends to forests dark and drear,
Sita steps before her husband wild and thorny paths to clear!

Like the tasted refuse water cast thy timid thoughts aside,
Take me to the pathless jungle, bid me by my lord abide,

Car and steed and gilded palace, vain are these to woman's life,
Dearer is her husband's shadow to the loved and loving wife!

For my mother often taught me and my father often spake,
That her home the wedded woman doth beside her husband make,

As the shadow to the substance, to her lord is faithful wife,
And she parts not from her consort till she parts with fleeting life!

Therefore bid me seek the jungle and in pathless forests roam,
Where the wild deer freely ranges and the tiger makes his home,

Happier than in father's mansions in the woods will Sita rove,
Waste no thought on home or kindred, nestling in her husband's love!

World-renowned is Rama's valor, fearless by her Rama's side,
Sita still will live and wander with a faithful woman's pride,

And the wild fruit she will gather from the fresh and fragrant wood,
And the food by Rama tasted shall be Sita's cherished food!

Bid me seek the sylvan greenwoods, wooded hills and plateaus high,
Limpid rills and crystal *nullas* as they softly ripple by,

And where in the lake of lotus tuneful ducks their plumage lave,
Let me with my loving Rama skim the cool translucent wave!

Years will pass in happy union,—happiest lot to woman given,—
Sita seeks not throne or empire, nor the brighter joys of heaven,

Heaven conceals not brighter mansions in its sunny fields of pride,
Where without her lord and husband faithful Sita would reside!

Therefore let me seek the jungle where the jungle-rangers rove,
Dearer than the royal palace, where I share my husband's love,

And my heart in sweet communion shall my Rama's wishes share
And my wifely toil shall lighten Rama's load of woe and care!"

Vainly gentle Rama pleaded dangers of the jungle life,
Vainly spoke of toil and trial to a true and tender wife. II. 27

Romesh Dutt

*****

33
City in Mourning

Ayodhya, great city, seems
Like the night itself, in the pitch of dark
Where only cats are awake and owls,
Where men and monkeys keep to cover.

It looks like a river drying up
So that its shallows heat too soon
And waterfowl must surface, fish
And crocodiles restlessly stir.

It looks like a ruined army, warriors
Fallen everywhere, armour
Broken, elephants fallen, horses
And chariots fallen, banners thrown down.

It looks like the tide at ebb, brushed back
By a calm breeze, utterly quiet,
After its hour of foam and roar,
After its highest lifting wave.

It looks like an altar given up
After the Soma has been pressed,
The sacrificial implements
Left here and there, the priests all gone.

It looks like a cow come into heat
But lacking the service of a bull
And standing, desolate, in the pen,
Refusing the offered new-cut grass.

It looks like a necklace with the stones
That made it precious all removed,
Stones whose lustre glittered out,
Perfectly round, the rarest kind.

It looks like earth shot from its base,
All of its goodness being spent,
Or a star plunged out of heaven,
All its radiance dimmed out.

It looks like a creeper shrivelled up,
Blackened by forest fire, a creeper
That in late spring, a mass of flowers,
Had addled all the hovering bees.

It looks like a densely clouded sky,
Cutting off the moon and stars.
The market place and shops are all
Shut up, the townsmen deep in gloom.

It looks like a drunken party, all
The drinkers departed, having left
Behind their refuse, a carpeting
Of broken cups, voided of wine.

It looks like the fallen bow of a warrior
Dropped off his shoulders when an arrow
Split it, a long and hefty bow
Whose helpless string is broken now.

It looks like a young mare, unsaddled,
Standing forlorn and riderless;
Its rider was a daring man
And will not mount the saddle now.

It looks like the sun when its great light
Is buried under blue-black clouds
And hidden there for many days
During the time of endless rain. II. 106

V.N. Misra, L. Nathan and S. Vatsyayan

❄❄❄❄❄

34
The Sandals

Tears nor sighs nor sad entreaty Rama's changeless purpose shook,
Till once more with hands conjoinéd Bharat to his elder spoke:

"Rama, true to royal mercy, true to duties of thy race,
Grant this favour to thy mother, to thy brother grant this grace,

Vain were my unaided efforts to protect our father's throne,
Town and hamlet, lord and tiller, turn to thee and thee alone!

Unto Rama, friends and kinsmen, chiefs and warriors, turn in pain,
And each city chief and elder, and each humble village swain,

Base thy empire strong, unshaken, on a loyal nation's will,
With thy worth and with thy valour serve thy faithful people still!"

Rama raised the prostrate Bharat to his ever-loving breast,
And in voice of tuneful *hansa* thus his gentle speech addrest:

"Trust me, Bharat, lofty virtue, strength and will to thee belong,
Thou could'st rule a world-wide empire in thy faith and purpose strong,

And our father's ancient min'sters, ever faithful, wise and deep,
They shall help thee with their counsel and thy ancient frontiers keep.

List! the Moon may lose his lustre, Himalaya lose his snow,
Heaving Ocean pass his confines surging from the caves below,

But the truth-abiding Rama will not move from promise given,
He hath spoke and will not falter, help him righteous Gods in heaven!"

Blazing like the Sun in splendour, beauteous like the Lord of Night,
Rama vowed his Vow of Duty, changeless in his holy might!

"Humble token," answered Bharat, "still I seek from Rama's hand,
Token of his love and kindness, token of his high command,

From thy feet cast forth those sandals, they shall decorate the throne,
They shall nerve my heart to duty and shall safely guard thy own,

They shall to a loyal nation absent monarch's will proclaim,
Watch the frontiers of the empire and the people's homage claim!

Rama gave the loosened sandals as his younger humbly prayed,
Bharat bowed to them in homage and his parting purpose said:

"Not alone will banished Rama barks and matted tresses wear,
Fourteen years the crownéd Bharat will in hermit's dress appear,

Henceforth Bharat dwells in palace guised as hermit of the wood,
In the sumptuous hall of feasting wild fruit is his only food,

Fourteen years shall pass in waiting, weary toil and penance dire,
Then, if Rama comes not living, Bharat dies upon the pyre!" II. 122.9-26

Romesh Dutt

*****

35
Winter in Panchavati

Came and passed the golden autumn in the forest's gloomy shade,
And the northern blasts of winter swept along the silent glade,

When the chilly night was over, once at morn the prince of fame
For his morning's pure ablutions to the Godavari came.

Meek-eyed Sita softly followed with the pitcher in her arms,
Gallant Lakshman spake to Rama of the Indian winter's charms:

"Comes the bright and bracing winter to the royal Rama dear,
Like a bride the beauteous season doth in richest robes appear,

Frosty air and freshening zephyrs wake to life each mart and plain,
And the corn in dewdrop sparkling makes a sea of waving green,

But the village maid and matron shun the freezing river's shore,
By the fire the village elder tells the stirring tale of yore!

With the winter's ample harvest men perform each pious rite,
To the Fathers long departed, to the Gods of holy might,

With the rite of *agrayana* pious men their sins dispel,
And with gay and sweet observance songs of love the women tell,

And the monarchs bent on conquest mark the winter's cloudless glow,
Lead their bannered cars and forces 'gainst the rival and the foe!

Southwards rolls the solar chariot, and the cold and widowed North
Reft of 'bridal mark' and joyance coldly sighs her sorrows forth,

Southward rolls the solar chariot, Himalaya, 'home of snow,'
True to name and appellation doth in whiter garments glow,

Southward rolls the solar chariot, cold and crisp the frosty air,
And the wood of flower dismantled doth in russet robes appear!

Star of Pushya rules December and the night with rime is hoar,
And beneath the starry welkin in the woods we sleep no more,

And the pale moon mist-enshrouded sheds a faint and feeble beam,
As the breath obscures the mirror, winter mist obscures her gleam,

Hidden by the rising vapour faint she glistens on the dale,
Like our sun-embrownéd Sita with her toil and penance pale!

Sweeping blasts from western mountains through the gorges whistle by
And the *saras* and the curlew raise their shrill and piercing cry,

Boundless fields of wheat and barely are with dewdrops moist and wet,
And the golden rice of winter ripens like the clustering date,

Peopled marts and rural hamlets wake to life and cheerful toil,
And the peaceful happy nations prosper on their fertile soil!

Mark the sun in morning vapours—like the moon subdued and pale—
Brightening as the day advances piercing through the darksome veil,

Mark his gay and golden lustre sparkling o'er the dewy lea,
Mantling hill and field and forest, painting bush and leaf and tree,

Mark it glisten on the green grass, on each bright and bending blade,
Lighten up the long drawn vista, shooting through the gloomy glade!

Thirst-impelled the lordly tusker still avoids the freezing drink,
Wild duck and the tuneful *hansa* doubtful watch the river's brink,

From the rivers wrapped in vapour unseen cries the wild curlew
Unseen rolls the misty streamlet o'er its sandbank soaked in dew,

And the drooping water-lily bends her head beneath the frost,
Lost her fresh and fragrant beauty and her tender petals lost!

Now my errant fancy wanders to Ayodhya's distant town,
Where in hermit's barks and tresses Bharat wears the royal crown,

Scorning regal state and splendour, spurning pleasures loved of yore,
Spends his winter day in penance, sleeps at night upon the floor,

Aye! perchance Sarayu's waters seeks he now, serene and brave,
As we seek, when dawns the daylight, Godavari's limpid wave!" III. 13

Romesh Dutt

*****

36
The Season of Rain

Nine months through the rays of the sun
The sky had held the rain in its womb
It drinks up the waters of the seas
And waters are born from it, transformed.

Just now it seems quite reasonable
To drape the sun in flower chains,
Climbing to heaven on the steps
Of lacquered clouds, scaled to the sun.

The sky seems bruised, its bandages—
Tufts of soft and fleecy clouds,
Moving from the ruddy dusk,
Coppery, silver just at their edge.

The sky seems lovesick, very pale,
With ashen clouds, his sighs the breezes,
The twilight glimmer like a stroke
Of sandal painted on his brow.

The wind, sprung form the womb of clouds,
Cool and good as lotus petals,
Scented with *Ketaka*, cupped
In your hands, can now be drunk.

The mountains, wrapped in cloudy deerskin,
Bearing the sacred thread of streams,
Their mastered breath the wind in caves,
Seem like sages at their thought.

Heaven is being flogged by whips
Of long gold lightning, and growls
Through the low bellowing of the clouds,
A wounded thing in agony.

The lightning that flashes the cloud's
Dark lap suddenly seems
To be my own miserable Sita
Struggling in Ravana's lap.

These horizons, dear to all
Who love, are buried now,
Smeared by a thickened paste of clouds,
The planets and the moon snuffed out.

Look at these *Kutaja* flowers
That blossom on the slopes of hills,
Some of them dimmed in smoky scud,
And shaking in their wish for rain.

These blossoms seem to quiet,
The desire I suffer with more desire.

The dust has fallen, the wind is cooling down,
The worst of summer done, the royal armies
Set to march, must wait at ease, and those
Far off begin their long processional home.

The herons with their mates are heading toward
Himalayan perches thrilling at their flight;
On muddy roads, oxcarts slide and sink,
Laboring in the drench of endless rain.

The sky, spread out with clouds, appears as one
Immense and quiet body of water, here,
Open and light, there dark, and there,
Suddenly blocked by clouds piled up like peaks.

Their waters mingled with the muddy ochre
Of the hills, mingled with the bloom
Of teak and of *Kadamba,* streams flash down
And peacocks echo them with liquid cries.

The clouds bellow them with their thunder everywhere,
Like great elephants shouldering through the front
Of battle, lightning for their oriflamme
And garlanded with strung-out flights of geese.
Their great bulks cresting like mountain tops.

That flock of geese, circling overhead,
Flies as if lashed ahead by lust for clouds;
It seems a wreath of snowy lotus meant
For heaven, trembling at those windy heights.

The forest glitters as the peacocks dance,
Kadamba trees lift up their gift of gold,
Bulls are swollen taut with their desire.
And the earth spreads out its shining crop of green. IV. 28

V.N. Misra, L. Nathan and S. Vatsyayan

*****

37
The Aśoka Garden

Crossed the ocean's boundless waters, Hanuman in duty brave,
Lighted on the emerald island girdled by the sapphire wave,

And in tireless quest of Sita searched the margin of the sea,
In a dark Aśoka garden hid himself within a tree.

Creepers threw their clasping tendrils round the trees of ample height,
Stately palm and feathered cocoa, fruit and blossoms pleased the sight,

Herds of tame and gentle creatures in the grassy meadow strayed,
Kokils sang in leafy thicket, birds of plumage lit the shade,

Limpid lakes of scented lotus with their fragrance filled the air,
Homes and huts of rustic beauty peeped through bushes green and fair,

Blossoms rich in tint and fragrance in the checkered shadow gleamed,
Clustering fruits of golden beauty in the yellow sunlight beamed!

Brightly shone the red *Aśoka* with the morning's golden ray,
Karnikāra and *Kinsuka* dazzling as the light of day,

Brightly grew the flower of *Champak* in the vale and on the reef,
Punnāga and *Saptaparna* with its seven-fold scented leaf,

Rich in blossoms many tinted, grateful to the ravished eye,
Gay and green and glorious Lanka was like garden of the sky,

Rich in fruit and laden creeper and in beauteous bush and tree,
Flower-bespangled golden Lanka was like gem-bespangled sea!

Rose a palace in the woodlands girt by pillars strong and high,
Snowy-white like fair Kailasa cleaving through the azure sky,

And its steps were ocean coral and its pavement yellow gold,
White and gay and heaven-aspiring rose the structure high and bold!

By the rich and royal mansion Hanuman his eyes did rest,
On a woman sad and sorrowing in her sylvan garments drest,

Like the moon obscured and clouded, dim with shadows deep and dark,
Like the smoke-enshrouded red fire, dying with a feeble spark,

Like the tempest-pelted lotus by the wind and torrent shaken,
Like the beauteous star Rohini by a *graha* overtaken!

Fasts and vigils paled her beauty, tears bedimmed her tender grace,
Anguish dwelt within her bosom, sorrow darkened on her face,

And she lived by Rakshas guarded, as a faint and timid deer,
Severed from her herd and kindred when the prowling wolves are near,

And her raven locks ungathered hung behind in single braid,
And her gentle eye was lightless, and her brow was hid in shade!

"This is she! the peerless princess, Rama's consort loved and lost,
This is she! the saintly Sita, by a cruel fortune crost,"

Hanuman thus thought and pondered: "On her graceful form I spy,
Gems and gold by sorrowing Rama oft depicted with a sigh,

On her ears the golden pendants and the tiger's sharpened tooth,
On her arms the jewelled bracelets, tokens of unchanging truth,

On her pallid brow and bosom still the radiant jewels shine,
Rama with a sweet affection did in early days entwine!

Hermit's garments clothe her person, braided is her raven hair,
Matted bark of trees of forest drape her neck and bosom fair,

And a dower of dazzling beauty still bedecks her peerless face,
Though the shadowing tinge of sorrow darkens all her earlier grace!

This is she! the soft-eyed Sita, wept with unavailing tear,
This is she! the faithful consort, unto Rama ever dear,

Unforgetting and unchanging, truthful still in deed and word,
Sita in her silent suffering sorrows for her absent lord,

Still for Rama lost but cherished, Sita heaves the choking sigh,
Sita lives for righteous Rama, for her Rama she would die!" V.15

Romesh Dutt

*****

AŚVAGHOSHA

Buddhacharita

38
The Great Departure

Thus the best of men, beautiful in form and shining like black-tracked Agni, instructed the white horse, the best of steeds, in his duty as though he were a friend, and mounted him to go to the forest, just as the sun, blazing like fire, mounts a white autumnal cloud.

Thereon the good horse suppressed all noise, that would seem terrifying in the night-time or might awaken the attendants; his jaws were soundless and he silenced his neighing, as he went forth with steady steps.

Then the Yakshas bowed down their bodies and bore up his hoofs off the ground with the tips of their hands, that thrilled with joy; their forearms were adorned with golden bands and their hands were like lotuses, so that they seemed to be throwing lotuses beneath him.

The city gatehouses, which were closed with gates furnished with heavy bars and which could not easily have been forced even by elephants, opened noiselessly of their own accord as the king's son passed along.

Then he went forth out of his father's city, in the firmness of his resolve quitting without concern his father, who was devoted to him, his young son, his affectionate people and his unequalled magnificence.

Thereon he, whose eyes were long like stainless lotuses born of the mud, looked back at the city and uttered a lion-roar: "I shall not be entering the city named after Kapila, till I have seen the further shore of life and death."

Hearing his words, the troops of the court of the Lord of Wealth rejoiced, and the hosts of gods with joyful minds foretold the fulfilment of his resolve.

Other heavenly beings of fiery forms recognized his purpose to be of the greatest difficulty and, like moon-beams piercing a rift in a cloud, produced a bright light on his frosty path.

But that steed, like a steed of the Sun, speeding on as if spurred in mind, and the prince travelled very many leagues, before the stars in the sky grew discoloured with the dawn.

Then the world's eye, the sun, rose in a moment, and the best of men saw the hermitage of the descendant of Bhrigu.

When he saw it with the deer sleeping in perfect trust and the birds sitting at peace, he felt, as it were, rested and as if the goal were attained.

In order to eschew arrogance and to show honour to asceticism, and in accordance with his politeness he dismounted from the horse.

And alighting, he patted his steed, saying, "Your task is accomplished", and well-pleased he said to Chandaka, bedewing him as it were with his eye:—

"In following this horse, whose speed is like that of Tārkshya you have shown, good friend, both loyalty to me and your own prowess.

Although I am entirely given up to other matters, I am gripped to the heart by you, who possess equally this devotion to your master in such a degree and also capability.

A man, though not devoted, may be capable, or though not capable, may be devoted; but it is hard to find in the world a man like you who is at the same time loyal and capable.

Therefore I am well-pleased with this your noble action in displaying towards me this feeling, which takes no count even of possible rewards.

Who would not be favourably disposed to a man in a position to reward him? In the opposite case even kinsfolk for the most part become strangers.

The son is cherished to continue the family; the father is honoured to obtain maintenance. The attachment of the world is always due to some motive. No feeling that this or that person is one's kin subsists without a cause.

Why speak many words? In short, you have done me a very great kindness. Return with the horse. I have arrived at the desired spot."

With these words the mighty prince unloosed his ornaments and gave them to Chandaka, whose mind smarted with sorrow, in order to do him benefit.

Taking from his diadem the blazing jewel, which performed the function of a light, he stood like mount Mandara with the sun on it, and uttered these words:—

"With this jewel, Chanda, you must make repeated obeisance to the king, and in order to abate his grief you must in full confidence give him this message from me:—

"I have entered the penance grove to put an end to birth and death, and not forsooth out of yearning for Paradise, or out of lack of affection or out of anger.

Therefore you should not grieve for me, since I have left my home for this purpose. For a union, however long it has lasted, in time will cease to be." V. 79-87 and VI. 1-16

E.H. Johnston

* * * * *

39
The Leave Taking

On hearing these words Chanda was overcome with anguish and, folding his hands, replied with a voice strangled with sobs:—

"At this disposition of yours, O my lord, which must cause distress to your kinsfolk, my mind sinks down like an elephant in the mud of a river.

To whom would not such a determination as this of yours cause tears, even if his heart were of iron, how much more when it is faltering with love?

For this delicacy of limb, fitted only for lying in a palace, is not compatible with the ground of the penance grove, covered by sharp blades of *darbha*-grass.

But as for my bringing this horse to you after hearing your resolve, it was some divine power, O my lord, that forcibly caused me to do it.

For if I had been in command of myself, how could I, on knowing this your resolve, have brought you the horse, the bale of Kapilavāstu?

Therefore, O mighty prince, you should not desert, as a nihilist the good Law, your loving aged father, who yearns so for his son.

Nor should you forget, like an ingrate kind treatment, the queen, your second mother, who exhausted herself in bringing you up.

You should not abandon, like a coward the sovereignty he has obtained, the virtuous princess, mother of a young son, devotedly faithful to her husband and of illustrious lineage.

You should not abandon, like a vicious man his excellent repute, the young son of Yaśodharā, worthy of praise and best of the cherishers of fame and *dharma.*

Or if, O my master, you are determined to abandon your father and your kingdom, you should not abandon me. For your feet are my sole refuge.

I cannot leave you in the forest, as Sumantra did Rāghava, and go to the city with burning heart."

The best of speakers heard these words of the grief-stricken Chanda and spoke to him, self-possessed and with the utmost firmness:—

"Quit this affliction, Chanda, over parting from me; separation is the fixed law among corporeal beings, in that they are subject to different births.

Should affection lead me not to quit my kinsfolk of myself, still death would part us one from the other against our wills.

My mother bore me in her womb with pains and great longing. Her efforts have been fruitless. What am I to her now or she to me?

As birds collect on the roosting tree and then go their separate ways again, so inevitably the union of beings ends in their parting.

And as the clouds come together and depart asunder again, so I deem the meeting and severance of creatures that draw breath.

Since such is the case then, my good friend, be not afflicted; go your way. But if your affection tarries, still go and then return again.

And you should say to the folk in Kapilavāstu, who keep regard for me, "Quit your love for him and hear his resolve.

Either, he says, he will quickly come back, after destroying birth and death; or, lacking in right effort and failing to reach the goal, he will perish." "

On hearing his speech, Kanthaka, the finest of steeds, licked his feet and shed scalding tears.

With his webbed hand, which was marked with svastikas and bore the wheel sign on the palm, the prince stroked Kanthaka and spoke to him as if he were his comrade of like age:—

"Do not shed tears, Kanthaka, you have displayed the qualities of a good horse. Be patient; this your toil will soon bring forth its fruit."

Then he resolutely took from Chanda's hand the sharp sword which had a jewelled hilt and was decorated with gold inlay, and drew it from the scabbard, as if he were drawing a snake from a hole.

Having unsheathed it with its blade dark blue as a blue lotus petal, he cut off his decorated headdress with the hair enclosed in it and tossed it with the muslin trailing from it into the air, as though tossing a goose into a lake.

And the inhabitants of Heaven caught it reverently, as it was thrown, with the intention of worshipping it, and the divine hosts paid it due adoration in Heaven with celestial honours.

Then he dismissed the weeping Chandaka and, wearing the ochre robe and bearing the fame of his steadfastness, moved majestically to where the hermitage was, resembling the monarch of the stars enveloped in a sunset cloud

Then when his master went thence to the penance grove in his discoloured clothes and free from desire for rule, the groom flung up his arms and, wailing bitterly, fell to the ground.

Looking back once more, he wept aloud and clasped the horse, Kanthaka, with his arms. Then in despair he lamented again and again and started for the city with his body, but not with his mind.

Sometimes he brooded and sometimes he lamented, sometimes he stumbled and sometimes he fell. So journeying in grief under the force of his devotion, he performed many actions on the road in complete abandon. VI. 25-36, 42-47, 50-57, 65-68.

E.H. Johnston

* * * * *

40
The Grief of Yaśodharā

But then up spoke Yaśodharā, her eyes reddened with anger, her voice choking with the bitterness born of despair, her bosom heaving with sighs, and tears streaming down with the grief she was enduring:—

"Where, Chandaka, has he gone, my heart's desire, after deserting me at night against my will while I slept? My mind trembles, when both you and Kanthaka have returned, while three went forth together.

Why do you weep here to-day, you brute, after doing me an ignoble, unkind, unfriendly deed? Hold back your tears, be contented in mind. Tears go ill with that deed of yours.

For through you, his loving obedient faithful good companion, always doing what is proper, my lord has gone never to return. Rejoice, by good fortune your toil is rewarded with success.

Better is it for a man to have a wise enemy than a silly friend, who is skilful only in the wrong way. For your imprudence and so-called friendship have wrought great ruin for this family.

For these princesses, with their ornaments laid aside and their eyes reddened and stained by incessant tears, are sorely to be pitied like widows whose splendour has departed, though their lord is still in existence as much as are the Himalayas or the earth.

And these rows of pavilions seems to weep together with the women, on separation from him, casting up their pinnacles for arms and heaving long sighs with their enamoured doves.

This horse Kanthaka too must have been desirous of my ruin in every way; for, when everyone was asleep at night, he thus carried off my treasure from here, like a jewel-thief.

Seeing that he is certainly able to stand up even to the strokes of the arrows that fall on him, not to speak of the whip, how was it he went off under fear of the fall of the whip, taking with him my good fortune and my heart together?

To-day the base creature neighs loudly, filling as it were the royal abode; but when he was carrying away my beloved, it was then that the wretched horse was dumb.

For if he had neighed and so woken up the people, or if he had made a noise with his hoofs, or if he had made the loudest sound he could with his jaws, such suffering would not have come on me."

If it is not to be my lot to look up at the sweetly-smiling long-eyed face of my lord, still is this poor Rāhula never to be dandled in his father's lap?

Alas! If my lord is tender in body and high in spirit, how cruel and exceeding hard is his mind, when in sooth he abandons such an infant son with his babbling talk, who would charm even an enemy.

My heart too is certainly exceeding hard, made of stone or even of iron, in that it does not break in its orphaned state, when my lord, accustomed to all pleasures, has departed to the forest without his royal glory." VIII. 31-34, 67-69

E.H. Johnston

*****

41
The Final Penance

He bathed and, as in his emaciation he came painfully up the bank of the Nairanjana, the trees growing on the slope bent low the tips of their branches in adoration to give him a helping hand.

At that time on divine instigation Nandabālā, the daughter of the cow herd chief, went there, joy bursting from her heart.

She was wearing a dark-blue cloth and her arms were brilliant with white shells, so that she seemed like Yamunā, best of rivers, when its dark-blue water is wreathed with foam.

Her delight was enhanced by faith, and her blue-lotus eyes opened wide, as, doing obeisance with her head, she caused him to accept milk rice.

By partaking of it he secured for her the full reward of her birth, and himself through the satisfaction of the six sense faculties became capable of obtaining enlightenment.

Then the sage's form together with his fame reached full roundness and he bore united in his single person the loveliness of the moon and the steadfastness of the ocean.

The five mendicants, holding that he had renounced the holy life, left him, as the five elements leave the thinking soul when it is liberated.

On this, with his resolution for sole companion, he made up his mind for enlightenment and proceeded to the root of a *pipal* tree, where the ground was carpeted with green grass.

Then at that moment Kāla, the best of serpents, whose might was as that of the king of elephants, was awakened by the incomparable sound of his feet, and, realizing that the great sage had determined on enlightenment, he uttered this eulogy:—

"Since, O sage, the earth thunders, as it were, again and again, as it is pressed by your feet, and since your splendour shines forth as of the sun, certainly you will today enjoy the desired result.

Since, O lotus-eyed one, the flocks of blue jays, circling in the air, proceed round you right-handed, and since gentle breezes blow in the sky, today without doubt you will become a Buddha."

Then, after the lordliest of serpents had thus extolled him, he took clean grass from a grass-cutter, and, betaking himself to the foot of the great pure tree, he made a vow for enlightenment and seated himself.

Then he took up the supreme, immovable cross-legged posture with his limbs massed together like the coils of a sleeping serpent, saying, "I will not rise form this position on the ground till I achieve the completion of my task".

Then when the Holy One took his seat with determined soul, the denizens of the heavens felt unequalled joy, and the birds and the companies of wild beasts refrained from noise nor did the forest trees, when struck by the wind, rustle at all. XII. 108-121

E.H. Johnston

* * * * *

42
The Army of Māra

Then as soon as Māra thought of his army in his desire to obstruct the tranquility of the Śākya sage, his followers stood round him, in various forms and carrying lances, trees, javelins, clubs and swords in their hands;

Having the faces of boars, fishes, horses, asses and camels, or the countenances of tigers, bears, lions and elephants, one-eyed, many-mouthed, three-headed, with pendulous bellics and speckled bellies;

Without knees or thighs, or with knees vast as pots, or armed with tusks or talons, or with skulls for faces, or with many bodies, or with half their faces broken off or with huge visages;

Ashy-grey in colour, tricked out with red spots, carrying ascetics' staves, with hair smoke-coloured like a monkey's, hung round with garlands, with pendent ears like elephants, clad in skins or entirely naked;

With half their countenances white or half their bodies green; some also copper-coloured, smoke-coloured, tawny or black; some too with arms having an overgarment of snakes, or with rows of jangling bells at their girdles;

Tall as toddy-palms and grasping stakes, or of the stature of children with projecting tusks, or with the faces of sheep and the eyes of birds, or with cat-faces and human bodies;

With dishevelled hair, or with topknots and half-shaven polls, clothed in red and with disordered headdresses, with bristling faces and frowning visages, suckers of the vital essence and suckers of the mind.

Some, as they ran, leapt wildly about, some jumped on each other; while some gambolled in the sky, others sped along among the treetops.

One danced about, brandishing a trident; another snorted, as he trailed a club; one roared like a bull in his excitement, another blazed fire from every hair.

Such were the hordes of fiends who stood encompassing the root of the *bodhi* tree on all sides, anxious to seize and to kill, and awaiting the command of their master.

Beholding in the beginning of the night the hour of conflict between Māra and the bull of the Śākyas, the sky lost its brightness, the earth shook and the quarters blazed and crashed.

The wind raged wildly in every direction, the stars did not shine, the moon was not seen, and night spread forth still thicker darkness and all the oceans were troubled. XIII. 18-29

E.H. Johnston

* * * * *

43
The Enlightenment

At that moment of the fourth watch, when the dawn came up and all that moves or moves not was stilled, the great seer reached the stage which knows no alteration, the sovereign leader the state of omniscience.

When, as the Buddha, he knew this truth, the earth swayed like a woman drunken with wine, the quarters shone bright with crowds Siddhas, and mighty drums resounded in the sky.

Pleasant breezes blew softly, the heaven rained moisture from a cloudless sky, and from the trees there dropped flowers and fruit out of due season as if to do him honour.

At that time, just as in Paradise, *māndārava* flowers, lotuses and water-lilies of gold and beryl fell from the sky and bestrewed the place of the Śākya sage.

At that moment none gave way to anger, no one was ill or experienced any discomfort, none resorted to sinful ways or indulged in intoxication of mind; the world became tranquil, as though it had reached perfection. XIV. 86-90

E.H. Johnston

* * * * *

BHĀSA

Svapna Vāsavadattā

44
Flight of Cranes

Straight sometimes, sometimes scattered, or curving,
Or, as they wheel, crooked as the Great Bear's fork,
Their flight gleams like a contour of the sky,
Pale as a snake's belly, its skin just shed. IV. 2

V.N. Misra, L. Nathan and S. Vatsyayan

*****

Chārudatta

45
Moonrise

The moonrise, pale as the dried date palm;
Comfort of young girls, lamp of the highway,
Its shine tumbles into the pits of dark
Like milk flooding the caking mud of pools I. 29

V.N. Misra, L. Nathan and S. Vatsyayan

*****

From Subhāshita Ratnakosha of Vidyākara

46
The Magic of Moonlight

The cat, thinking its rays are milk,
licks them from the dish;
the elephant, seeing them woven through the lattice of the trees,
takes them for lotus stems;

the damsel after love would draw them from her couch
   as if they were her dress:
see how the moon in its pride of light
has cozened all the world. 905

D.H.H. Ingalls

❄❄❄❄❄

47
End of the Rains

The sun gives sharp pain
like a low man newly rich.
The deer drops his horns
like a thankless friend.
The waters grow lucid
like a saint's pious thought;
and the mud is squeezed dry
like a poor man who keeps a mistress 276

D.H.H. Ingalls

❄❄❄❄❄

HĀLA

Gāthā Sattasai

48
Verses

1

Distance destroys love,
So does the lack of it:
Gossip destroys love,
And sometimes
It takes nothing
To destroy love. 81

2

His form
In my eyes,
His touch
In my limbs,
His words
In my ears,
His heart
In my heart:
Now who's
Separated? 132

3

As the traveller, eyes raised,
Cupped hands filled with water, spreads
His fingers and lets it run through,
She pouring it reduces the trickle 161

4

The way he stared,
I kept covering my self,
Not that I wanted him
To look elsewhere. 73

5

As the bridegroom
    Feigning sleep
Sidles towards her,
    Her thighs stiffen and swiftly
With trembling hand
    She clasps the knot. 648

6

Before the white jasmine
    Could unfold, impetuous bee,
You've mangled it. 444

7

In her first labour,
    She tells her friends,
'I won't let him
    Touch me again' They laugh. 123

8

With a bored smile
    Giving him a jujube berry
Marked with their son's first bite,
    'Look at this, 'she said. 200

9

Scared of the barber, the child bolts
    And behind him his mother,
Hair pushed back, skirt hitched, runs. 291

10

Let faithful wives
    Say what they like,
I don't sleep with my husband
    Even when I do. 888

11

Afraid of midday heat,
    Even your shadow
Strays under your feet:
    Come into the shade, traveller. 49

12

Wings hanging down, necks drawn in,
Sitting on fences as though spitted,
Crows get soaked in the rain. 564

13

Buffalos look back
And say goodbye to the grove,
As butchers, long knives in hand,
Take them away. 682

14

The moment it meets a bowstring,
The simple arrow's in flight:
Can the straight be friends
With the bent? 424

Arvind Krishna Mehrotra

15

How she scolded him,
The traveller, last might,
Handing straw out for his bed.
This morning, picking up the pieces,
How she weeps. 379

Edwin Gerow and Peter Dent

* * * * *

ŚŪDRAKA

Mricchakaṭika

49
The Storm

The sky, flung with piling clouds worked by the wind
To wild and shifty shapes, seems like frescoed wall;
Now they are herons pairing, now a flight of swans,
Now fish and crocodiles rolled by the sea, now towered castles.

Clouds, dark as wet leaves have soaked up the sun;
Anthills, collapsed by rain, go down like elephants showered with
arrows;
Lightning flares like a lamp that someone bears up and down in a
mansion;
The moonlight was carried off like the wife of a helpless man.

At Indra's command, the clouds
Hoist up the earth with chords of streaming silver;
Like elephants harnessed with lightning,
They heave and shoulder against each other.

Treble on palm leaf, bass on shrubs,
Sharp on stones, soft on ponds,
The rain beats out its music, a Vina,
Its chords plucked by an accomplished hand. V.

V.N. Misra, L. Nathan and S. Vatsyayan

Thundercloud, I think you are wicked.
You know I'm going to meet my own lover,
And yet you first scare me with your thunder,
And now you're trying to caress me
With your rain-hands. V.28

John Brough

❄❄❄❄❄

50
On Being Poor

Ah, Poverty, I mourn for your sad fate.
So long ago you claimed me as your friend,
And ever since you have been my constant guest.
Where will you find a home when I am dead? I.38

John Brough

I am not saddened by the loss of riches,
For riches flows in and out with turns of luck.
This is what hurts: the golden prop removed,
Friendships grow suddenly feeble, start to totter. I.13

V.N. Misra, L. Nathan and S. Vatsyayan

❄❄❄❄❄

VISHNU ŚARMĀ

Panchatantra

51
Kings

In sensuous coil
And heartless toil,
In sinuous course
And armoured force,
In savage harms
That yield to charms—
In all these things
Are the snakes like kings.

Uneven, rough,
And high enough—
Yet low folk roam
Their flanks as home,
And wild things haunt
Them, hungry, gaunt—
In all these things
Are hills like kings.

The things that claw, and the things that gore
Are unreliable things;
And so is a man with a sword in his hand,
And rivers, and women, and kings. I. 52-54

Arthur W. Ryder

* * * * *

52
The Penalty of Virtue

The fruit-tree's branch by very wealth
   Of fruit is bended low;
The peacock's feathered pride compels
   A sluggish gait and slow;
The blooded horse that wins his race,
Must like a cow be led:
The good in goodness often find
   An enemy to dread.

Where Jumna's waves roll blue
With sands of sapphire hue,
Black serpents have their lair;
And who would hunt them there,
But that a jewel's bright star
From each hood gleam afar?
By virtue rising, all
By that same virtue fall.

The man of virtue commonly
   Is hateful to the king,
While riches to the scamps and fools
   Habitually cling:
The ancient chant "By virtue great
   Is man" has run to seed;
The world takes rare and little note
   Of any plucky deed.

I. 297-99

Arthur W. Ryder

* * * * *

53
Fate

Success complete
In any feat
Is sure to bless
True manliness,
Man's effort (sufficiently great)
Is just what dullards call fate. V.30

Arthur W. Ryder

❄❄❄❄❄

54
True Friendship

'Tis hard to find in life
A friend, a bow, a wife,
Strong, supple to endure,
In stock and sinew pure,
In time of danger sure.

False friends are common. Yes, but where
True nature links a friendly pair,
The blessing is as rich as rare.

To bitter ends
You trust true friends,
Not wife nor mother,
Not son nor brother.

No long experience alloys
True friendship's sweet and supple joys;
No evil men can steal the treasure;
'Tis death, death only, sets a measure. II. 99-102

Arthur W. Ryder

❄❄❄❄❄

55
Fool and False

With the shrewd and upright man
    Seek a friendship rare;
Exercise with shrewd and false
    Superheedful care;
Pity for the upright fool
    Find within your heart;
If a man be fool and false,
    Shun him from the start. III. 96

Arthur W. Ryder

❄❄❄❄❄

56
Poverty

A beggar to the graveyard hied
And there "Friend corpse, arise," he cried;
"One moment lift my heavy weight
Of poverty; for I of late
Grow weary, and desire instead
Your comfort; you are good and dead."
The corpse was silent. He was sure
'Twas better to be dead than poor. V.18

Arthur W. Ryder

❄❄❄❄❄

57
Procrastination

The negligent who say:
'Some day, some other day—
The thing is pretty small;
Demands no thought at all,'
Are headed, heedless, straight
For that repentant state
That ever comes too late. III. 130

Arthur W. Ryder

❄❄❄❄❄

KĀLIDĀSA

Meghadūta

58
The Yaksha's City

Where palaces in much may rival thee—
Their ladies gay, thy lightning's dazzling powers—
Symphonic drums, thy thunder's melody—
Their bright mosaic floors, thy silver showers—
Thy rainbow, paintings, and thy height, cloud-licking towers.

Where the autumn lotus in dear fingers shines,
And lodh-flowers' April dust on faces rare,
Spring amaranth with winter jasmine twines
In women's braids, and summer siris fair,
The rainy madder in the parting of their hair.

Where men with maids whose charm no blemish mars
Climb to the open crystal balcony
Inlaid with flower-like sparkling of the stars,
And drink the love-wine from the wishing-tree,
And listen to the drums' deep-thundering dignity.

Where maidens whom the gods would gladly wed
Are fanned by breezes cool with Ganges' spray
In shadows that the trees of heaven spread;
In golden sands at hunt-the-pearl they play,
Bury their little fists, and draw them void away.

Where lovers' passion-trembling fingers cling
To silken robes whose sashes flutter wide,
The knots undone; and red-lipped women fling,
Silly with shame, their rouge from side to side,
Hoping in vain the flash of jewelled lamps to hide.

Where, brought to balconies' palatial tops
By ever-blowing guides, were clouds before
Like thee who spotted paintings with their drops;

Then, touched with guilty fear, were seen no more,
But scattered smoke-like through the lattice' grated door.

Where from the moonstones hung in nets of thread
Great drops of water trickle in the night—
When the moon shines clear and thou, O cloud, are fled—
To case the languors of the women's plight
Who lie relaxed and tired in love's embraces tight.

Where lovers, rich with hidden wealth untold,
Wander each day with nymphs for ever young,
Enjoy the wonders that the gardens hold,
The Shining Gardens, where the praise is sung
Of the god of wealth by choirs with love-impassioned tongue.

Where sweet nocturnal journeys are betrayed
At sunrise by the fallen flowers from curls
That fluttered as they stole along afraid,
By leaves, by golden lotuses, by pearls,
By broken necklaces that slipped from winsome girls. II. 1-9

Arthur W. Ryder

❄❄❄❄❄

59
The Yaksha's Message

As thou wouldst wake the jasmine's budding wonder,
Wake her with breezes blowing mistily;
Conceal thy lightnings, and with words of thunder
Speak boldly, though she answer haughtily
With eyes that fasten on the lattice and on thee.

'Thou art no widow; for thy husband's friend
Is come to tell thee what himself did say—
A cloud with low, sweet thunder-tones that send
All weary wanderers hastening on their way,
Eager to loose the braids of wives that lonely stay.'

Say this, and she will welcome thee indeed,
Sweet friend, with a yearning heart's tumultuous beating
And joy-uplifted eyes; and she will heed
The after message: such a friendly greeting
Is hardly less to woman's heart than lovers' meeting.

Thus too, my king, I pray of thee to speak,
Remembering kindness is its own reward;
'Thy lover lives, and from the holy peak
Asks if these absent days good health afford—
Those born to pain must ever use this opening word.

With body worn as thine, with pain as deep,
With tears and ceaseless longings answering thine,
With sighs more burning than the sighs that keep
Thy lips ascorch—doomed far from thee to pine,
He too doth weave the fancies that thy soul entwine.

He used to love, when women friends were near,
To whisper things he might have said aloud
That he might touch thy face and kiss thine ear;
Unheard and even unseen, no longer proud,
He now must send this yearning message by a cloud.

"I see thy limbs in graceful-creeping vines,
Thy glances in the eyes of gentle deer,
Thine eyebrows in the ripple's dancing lines,
Thy locks in plumes, thy face in moonlight clear—
Ah, jealous! But the whole sweet image is not here.

And when I paint that loving jealousy
With chalk upon the rock, and my caress
As at thy feet I lie, I cannot see
Through tears that to mine eyes unbidden press—
So stern a fate denies a painted happiness.

And when I toss mine arms to clasp thee tight,
Mine own though but in visions of a dream—
They who behold the oft-repeated sight,
The kind divinities of wood and stream,
Let fall great pearly tears that on the blossoms gleam.

Himalaya's breeze blows gently from the north,
Unsheathing twigs upon the deodar
And sweet with sap that it entices forth—
I embrace it lovingly; it came so far,
Perhaps it touched thee first, my life's unchanging star!

Oh, might the long, long night seem short to me!
Oh, might the day his hourly tortures hide!
Such longings for the things that cannot be,
Consume my helpless heart, sweet-glancing bride,
In burning agonies of absence from thy side.

Yet much reflection, dearest, makes me strong,
Strong with an inner strength; nor shouldst thou feel
Despair at which has come to us of wrong;
Who has unending woe or lasting weal?
Our fates move up and down upon a circling wheel.

When Vishnu rises from his serpent bed
The curse is ended; close thine eyelids tight
And wait till only four months more are sped;
Then we shall taste each long-desired delight
Through nights that the full autumn moon illumines bright.

And one thing more: thou layest once asleep,
Clasping my neck, then wakening with a scream;
And when I wondered why, thou couldst but weep
A while, and then a smile began to beam:
'Rogue! Rogue! I saw thee with another girl in dream.'

This memory shows me cheerful, gentle wife;
Then let no gossip thy suspicions move:
They say the affections strangely forfeit life
In separation, but in truth they prove
Toward the absent dear, a growing bulk of tenderest love." '

II 35-49

Arthur W. Ryder

*****

Kumārasambhava

60
The Bride's Adornment

Dusted with lodhra powder to remove the oil from her skin
tinged gold by the partly dry paste of sandalwood,
the women wrapped around her a cloth right for being bathed,
and led Umā to a four-pillared sunken bath.

Its floor paved with slabs of lapis lazuli
was inlaid in intricate patterns of pearls.
There they bathed Umā, pouring water from jars of gold,
while pipes sounded auspicious music.

Bright, flawlessly pure after her ritual bath,
and dressed in fresh wedding garments, she shone
Like the rich earth gleaming rain-sprinkled
and mantled in full-blown kāśa blossoms.

Chaste women winding their arms round Umā
then led her to a seat under a canopy
raised on four jewelled pillars, at the midpoint of which
was the altar where the Sacred Fire was kindled.

Seating that slender girl facing east, the women
delayed for some time, sitting before her,
the adornments ready beside them, their eyes
charmed by the vision of beauty in its pristine state.

Her gorgeous mass of hair dried by the smoke of incense
had flowers folded within it and tied by a woman
with a string of pale yellow madhūka blossoms
and green dūrva shoots into a charming chignon.

They smoothed cream of white aloe all over her body
and drew on it designs in yellow and gold pigments.
And she glowed in beauty surpassing Triple-Streamed Gangā
gleaming with sandy banks dotted with chakravāka birds.

Framed in charming curls, the splendour of her face
outshone the glory of a lotus with bees clinging,
or of the moon's bright orb fringed by wisps of clouds,
so that all talk of comparisons was cut short as vain.

The barley shoot placed at her ear held all eyes captive
and appeared to greatest advantage against her cheek,
translucent from the lodhra's bracing lotion
enhancing the brilliant pale gold gorochana.

The lower lip of that girl so exquisitely formed,
a line dividing it in the middle, its redness heightened
by a touch of beeswax, and pulsing expectant
of the fruit of its charm soon to come-Ah! how indescribable!

When a friend having tinted her feet with lāksha juice
and blessed her, said laughing: 'With this foot
may you touch the moon on your lord's head,'
without a word, Umā struck her with a garland.

Seeing as her eyes were exquisitely lovely
as the petals of some fine blue lotus, the women
adorning Umā applied the collyrium
not to enhance their brilliance, but only
because it was an auspicious mark to put on the bride.

Like a vine burgeoning with blossoms,
like the night when stars are rising,
like a stream on which chakravākas are gliding,
she gleamed wondrous as they adorned her with jewels.

And gazing at herself so gorgeous in the mirror's oval,
Umā of long eyes, stilled, could hardly wait
for Śiva's arrival. To be seen by her beloved
is a woman's reward for adorning herself, is it not? VII. 9-22

Chandra Rajan

*****

61
Omens of War

A fearful flock of evil birds,
  ready for the joy of eating the army of demons,
flew over the host of the gods,
  and clouded the sun.

A wind continually fluttered their umbrellas and banners,
  and troubled their eyes with clouds of whirling dust,
so that the trembling horses and elephants
  and the great chariots could not be seen.

Suddenly monstrous serpents, as black as powdered soot,
  scattering poison from their upraised heads,
frightful in form,
  appeared in the army's path.

The sun put on a ghastly robe
  of great and terrible snakes, curling together,
as if to mark his joy
  at the death of the enemy demon.

And before the very disc of the sun
  jackals bayed harshly together,
as though eager fiercely to lap the blood
  of the king of the foes of the gods, fallen in battle.

Lighting heaven from end to end,
  with flames flashing all around,
with an awful crash, rending the heart with terror,
  a thunderbolt fell from a cloudless sky.

The sky poured down torrents of red-hot ashes,
  with which were mixed blood and human bones,
till the flaming ends of heaven were filled with smoke
  and bore the dull hue of the neck of an ass.

Like the thundered threat of the angry death-god
  a great crash broke the walls of the ears,
a shattering sound, tearing the tops of the mountains,
  and wholly filling the belly of heaven.

The host of the foe was jostled together.
    The great elephants stumbled, the horses fell,
and all the footmen clung together in fear,
    as the earth trembled and the ocean rose to shake the mountains.

And, before the host of the foes of the gods,
    dogs lifted their muzzles to gaze on the sun,
Then, howling together with cries that rent the eardrums,
    they wretchedly slunk away. XV. 14-24

A.L. Basham

* * * * *

62
Advent of Spring and Love

And then within these mountain-forest reaches,
Skilled to distract saints' thoughts from heaven above
The young awakening Spring now yawns and stretches,
Belov'd companion of the god of love.

While the hot sun, untimely, came to waken
The North to be his love, the gentle South
Exhaled a sigh, thus to have been forsaken,
A breath warm-scented from her fragrant mouth.

The Ashoka then, its trunk and branches laden,
Full-flowered, with foil of many a green leaf-shoot,
Impatient, quite forgot to expect a maiden
To wake its flowers with anklet-tinkling foot.

On every blossom-arrow he created,
Feathered with leaves and tipped with mango-flame,
The fletcher Spring the owner designated,
Writing with bees the god of love's own name.

The Karnikāra's blossom, brightly glowing,
While by its scentlessness it grieved the mind,
Showed how God's will is set against bestowing
All excellences in one place combined.

Curved like the crescent moon, deep crimson traces
Glowed as Palāsha-buds began to swell,
As if the nail-marks of the Spring's embraces
Flushed on the forest-lands he loved so well.

Spring's Loveliness, with woman's wiles acquainted,
With flowers of Tilaka adorned her head,
Made beauty-spots of clinging bees, and painted
Fresh mango-blossom lips with morning-red.

Piyāla-blossom clusters shed their pollen
In smoke-clouds; and the deer, bewildered, blind,
Through forest-glades where rustling leaves had fallen,
Made rash by springtime, coursed against the wind.

The cuckoo's song, hoarsened to gentle cooing,
When food of mango-sprouts tightened his throat,
Became the voice of Love, to work the undoing
Of maids cold-hearted, by its magic note.

The fairy-women, with their winter faces
Devoid of lipstick, saw their colour fade,
While with the Spring the rising sweat left traces,
Smearing the beauty-marks so carefully made.

When, in the forest of their meditation,
The holy hermits saw the untimely spring,
Their minds were hard-pressed to resist temptation,
To keep their thoughts from Love's imagining.

When Love came there, his flower-bow ready stringing,
With fair Desire, his consort, at his side,
The forest creatures showed the passion springing
In every bridegroom's heart towards his bride.

From the same flower-cup which his love had savoured
The black bee sipped the nectar as a kiss;
While the black doe, by her own consort favoured,
Scratched by his antlers, closed her eyes in bliss.

The elephant with water lotus-scented
Sprayed her own lord, giving of love a token;
The wheel-drake, honouring his wife, presented
A half-chewed lotus-stalk which he had broken.

When nectar-wine had set her eyes a-dancing,
And sweat had smudged the fairy's painted face,
Her fairy-lover found her more entrancing
And checked his song to seek a fresh embrace.

When trembling petal-lips made laughing faces,
And blossom-breasts the slender stems were bending,
Even the forest-trees received the embraces
Of creeper-wives, from their bough-arms depending.

Yet Shiva still remained in meditation
Absorbed, although he heard the singing elves:
Can anything have power of perturbation
Of souls completely masters of themselves?

Then at the doorway of his forest dwelling
With rod of gold his servant Nandi stood,
Frowning, with finger to his lip, thus quelling
The unseemly conduct in the springtime wood.

Throughout the forest, at his simple stricture,
Dumb were the birds, and silent were the bees:
As in a scene fixed in a painted picture,
Stilled were the deer and motionless the trees. III. 24-42

John Brough

*****

Raghuvaṃśa

63
The Foresaken City

My desolate halls, my terraced houses,
Once handsome, masterless now, and wasting;
I seem to mimic the sun at its fall—
A wreckage of light through wind-slashed clouds.

These streets that lived with the anklets' trill
As they flashed toward love, now echo the patter
And yelp of jackals dribbling live ash
From their smoking tongues as they shadow on by.

Playful women, splashing, could sound
My pools like *mridangas*—a mellow thrum.
And now the water bellows and groans
Gored by the untamed buffalo's horns.

The bower poles snapped, the peacocks sit
In the trees. No dance. The *mridanga* is still.
Their tails, like the tails of their wilder kin,
Mere stubble, charred in the burning woods.

Pretty footprints on every stone,
Crimson of lac wherever they stepped.
Now a different red, printing the paw
Of a tiger gone by, just off the kill.

Cubs of the lion have clawed in their fury
The heads of those elephants painted at play
In a pool. The cows hold delicately out
Those silky lotus stems to their bulls.

The carved women who hold up these pillars
Are weathered into the rocky gray.
Skins that the snakes have left behind them
Glisten like new wraps at their breasts.

The moon no longer drops strings of pearl
On my houses of pleasure. They're patched with dark;
The plaster, exhausted, has dropped; moss thickens,
And grass has wedged out of every crack.

My vines, whose limbs were bent gently down
By women, at play, in their need for flowers,
Are torn apart now and snapped by a rage
Of monkeys, like savage alien folk.

Incense no longer drifts through the lattice
Of balcony windows—spiders have woven
Where lamps once lustred intensely the dark
And lovely young faces dawned on the day. XVI.11-20

V.N. Misra, L. Nathan and S. Vatsyayan

❄❄❄❄❄

Ritusaṃhāra

64
The Pageant of the Seasons

Summer

The furious sun is ablaze,
One longs for the moon,
The pools of limpid waters
Invite a dip evermore.
The twilight hours are charming
When the day dies down,
And Cupid, churner of the mind, is weary,
This, my love, is the advent of full Summer. 1.1

Rains

The approaching season of Rain, dear love,
Comes like a king in pride of power,
The rain-laden clouds are its rutting war-elephants;
The lambent flashes of lightning

Serve for its streaming pennons,
And the reverberating thunder
Is the rattle of its battle-drums;
It is hailed by a host of lovers
As the royal cavalcade is acclaimed
By crowds of suppliants. 2.1

Autumn

Behold! The Lady Autumn comes
Clad in the silver kasa blossoms,
Her fair visage is the white lotus bloom,
The tinkling of her anklet bells is heard
In the tuneful cry of wild geese on high;
The harvest of rice with ripening sheaves,
Bending in billows in the fresh young breeze,
Is her graceful figure and supple body;
She emulates the charming bride
With white bridal vesture and lily-white face,
The jingling anklets and slender figure,
And the shoulders bowed with decorous modesty
And woman's gentle grace. 3.1

Early Winter

Behold! The young maid, mirror in hand,
Making up her lotus face
In the sidelong morning sun;
Pouting her mouth she scans her lips
Whose essence was sucked by the lover. 4.13

Winter

May this winter time
Rich in dainties, sweets and lucent syrups,
Charming with the fields of rice,
And cloying with the juice of the sugarcane,
Warm with love's awakening
And happy fulfilment,
But painful to pining lovers,
Tend to your bliss for ever! 5.16

Spring

The trees aflower are crowned with glory,
The waters are strewn with lotus and lily,
The balmy breeze liberates fragrance,
And maidens are filled with dreams of love;
The languid perfection of the day
Wanes to a quivering twilight,
And all that breathes, or moves, or blossoms
Is sweeter, my love, in Spring. 6.2

R.S. Pandit

* * * * *

Abhijnānaśākuntala

65
Remembrances of Shakuntala

I cannot know whom Fate shall once
Permit to own this faultless form,
A bloom whose perfume none has drunk.
A bud by human hand uncut,
A pure, unperforated pearl,
Fresh honey not by mortal sipped,
The perfect fruit of holy deeds.

She looked aside before my gaze;
She smiled, but with a feigned pretense;
And so, by coyness checked, her love
Was half concealed and half revealed.

The tender girl was hardly gone
When by pretense she stopped and cried:
"A Kusha grass has stung my foot!"
And gazed around, and feigned to free
Her robe, as if by brambles caught.

When in the midst of happy hours
A fervent longing fills our heart,
As we behold enchanting forms,
Or hear delightful music sound,
It is then our soul with vague,
But lingering, love remembers yet
The affections of a former life. II. 10-12, V.2

A. Hjalmar Edgren

* * * * *

Vikramorvaśīya

66
The Search for Urvaśi

Peacock, I beg you to tell me this thing:
while roaming the grove did you see my love?
Listen! A wild goose gait and a face like the moon—
by the signs that I've told you you'll know her.

O blue-necked bird, in this grove
the long white neck
of my love is raised in longing.
O white-eyed bird, the sight of
her long blue eyes
would be worthy of your waiting.

Gentle winds part tail feathers, black
and glossy as lightning-streaked clouds;
because my love has disappeared,
the peacock's plumage has no rival.
Her thick hair is adorned with flowers,
the ribbon loosened for sweet love play—
if she were here now, would a peacock
dare to compete. IV. 20-22

David Gitomer

* * * * *

67
Signs of Urvaśi

Oh joy! I see a hint of her. This way
Then went her angry beauty! Lo, her bodice
Bright green as is a parrot's belly, smitten
With crimson drops. It once veiled in her bosom
And paused to show her navel deep as love.
These are her tears that from those angry eyes
Went trickling, stealing scarlet from her lips
To spangle all this green. Doubtless her heaving
Tumult of breasts broke its dear hold and, she
Stumbling in anger, from my heaven it drifted. IV.7

Sri Aurobindo

❄ ❄ ❄ ❄ ❄

68
Twilight

How beautifully twilight sits and dreams
Upon these palace walls! The peacocks now
Sit on their perches, drowsed with sleep and night,
Like figures hewn in stone. And on the roof
The fluttering pigeons with their pallid wings
Mislead the eye, disguised as rings of smoke
That from the window-ways have floated out
Into the evening... III.2

Sri Aurobindo

❄ ❄ ❄ ❄ ❄

ŚYĀMILAKA

Pādatāḍitaka

69
On Laughter

Ascetics do not attain 'release' by weeping,
humorous stories do not obstruct a future heaven;
Therefore a wise man should laugh with an appreciative mind
after abandoning mean modes of life. V.5

A.K. Warder

* * * * *

SUBANDHU

Vāsavadattā

70
Villains

Villains have extremely subtle understanding
   but only of very dark deeds;
For the eyes of owls see their objects
   only in darkness.

The more a villain, dark with cunning,
   outrages a good man,
As a dark hand with ashes passes over a mirror,
   the more he makes him of spotless lustre. V. 7-8

A.K. Warder

*****

BHĀRAVI

Kirātārjunīya

71
The Water Sport

The colour washed from their cheeks, the lac from their lips,
Collyrium gone, and still they shone, most lovely,
And seeing them shine, their lovers lucidly knew
That beauty lent the gauds it wore all their beauty.

Swaying lotus matched with glowing face,
Shifting line of foam with swinging necklace,
Bright water with the skin this water rinsed—
The waves strove with their beauty, strove and lost.

Their half-closed eyes send out a long look
To lovers, who hold them trembling, very close;
Their breasts lift in the water; they're breathing deep—
From weariness, or a high tide of desire?

The water, broken by the slow advance
Of breasts, of hips, of thighs, like stately prows
Scampered ahead, in ripples, to the shore—
Crying that the play of goddesses is done.

Its blue stained by sandalwood washed off
And spreading; its surface streaked with tangled garlands,
Its sinking waves a rumpled sheet—with the women gone
The river seemed a beautifully tousled marriage bed. VIII

V.N. Misra, L. Nathan and S. Vatsyayan

*****

72
Of Fools

To quarrel with them is a loss of face;
To have their friendship is a sad disgrace:
A man of sterling judgement realizes
What fools are worth, and foolish men despises. XIV

John Brough

* * * * *

73
In Praise of Good Words

Lucid, cleanly uttered, and good to hear,
Winning even a mind that came to attack;
Straight, fluent, but also grave with sense,
A speech issuing from act on scrupulous act.

There are those, it's true, so facile and well-schooled
Their talk exactly proclaims their adequate minds;
And then a few, a masterly few, whose words
Flash, of a sudden, down through the dark of sense.

Some find powerful plainness is best, and some
Allusion, finely worked until it's exact;
Different stations, different tastes. Most coveted
And rare the speech that lifts all men to its praise. XIV

V.N. Misra, L. Nathan and S. Vatsyayan

* * * * *

MĀGHA

Śiśupālavadha

74
The Carousal

Beautifully adorned and richly scented,
Shining with restless lotus eyes, the faces
Of these cherished girls had such round lips,
Their lovers used red mouths as cups for wine.

Netting down shyness with their warm attentions,
Rousing by their desires the girls' desires,
The young men made them forget all shame and drink
Their very love, deeply disguised as wine.

A mirror for the lover's lovely face,
And perfumed with freshly gathered mango-buds,
And sweet, and hummed over by bees, and cool,
The wine left all the senses satisfied.

The drunken bee hovered, confused between
The wide-cyed faces of these girls who breathed out
The sweet bouquet of wine they drank and the cups
They held figured with lotuses carved like life.

The wine, tasted by the lips of women
So lovely, surely acquired a richer taste,
For though their lovers had tasted the same before,
This was new, more sweet, till now untasted. X

V.N. Misra, L. Nathan and S. Vatsyayan

❄❄❄❄❄

75
The Morning After

The bride of the East, at last and with ease, discards
The veil of moonlight she held so close for so long—
A gauze of shyness that, finally let slip, discloses
A face that glows with the wine of the morning sun.

Having watched all night with wide-eyed attention the marvel
Of the always-novel play of loving pairs,
The flame of the lamp now wavers, flutters, and dulls
Like an eye that, open too long, is glazing with sleep.

Night, like a woman done with a secret tryst,
Hurries away, her raiment the dappled sky
Crumpled with the moon's long work, the breeze
Of dawn made aromatic by their loving.

The directions haul up the sun from the sea like women
Hauling a bulky pitcher out of a well.
The rays are laid like a spread of ropes being lowered,
The chatter of birds like women's noisy gossip.

The golden wine cup earlier drained by the girls,
In their revels now seems to be—
Tinted by the new red rays of the dawn,
Filled to the top again, brimming with wine. XI

V.N. Misra, L. Nathan and S. Vatsyayan

*****

76
The Island City of Dvārakā

Circled by sea, the four directions
Glowing gold from its golden walls,
The city rose from the waves rejoicing,
Bright as the blaze at the ocean's heart.

Circled by conchs that tossed in the waves
Of the restless sea, the fortified walls
Of the city seemed like Sumeru's peak
Crowned at night by the wheeling stars.

The sea, stacking wave above wave,
Sweeping in the jewels that traders
Had piled on their wharves, earned once more
Its old name: The Treasury of Gems.

And yet the sea, with waves for hands,
Has carefully set out those jewels,
Still dripping wet, on the city's doorsteps,
As if to dry them in the sun.

The waves come plunging from far off,
Set to subdue the towering walls.
Their power repulsed, they fall away,
Beaten and shamed, and melt to nothing.

A cloud, wanting to see the wonder,
But suddenly checked by battlement,
Roars out in rage, but then begins
To weep, disguising its tears as rain.

At night, the marble stairs and crystal
Terraces of mansions merge
With moonlight, so Dvārakā's women seem
Like Heaven's girls strolling the sky. III

V.N. Misra, L. Nathan and S. Vatsyayan

*****

BHARTRIHARI

Śatakatrayam

77
Verses on Life

One cloak in ignorance absolutely fits;
Justly if worn, some grace is even lent;
Silence in sessions of the learned sits
On the fool's brow like a bright ornament. 6

When I was with a little knowledge cursed,
Like a mad elephant I stormed about
And thought myself all-knowing. But when deep versed
Rich minds some portion of their wealth disbursed
My poverty to raise, then for a lout
And dunce I knew myself, and the insolence went
Out from me like a fever violent. 7

It is not armlets that adorn a man,
Nor necklaces all crammed with moonbright pearls,
Nor baths, nor ointments, nor arrangéd curls.
'Tis art of excellent speech that only can
Adorn him; jewels perish, garlands fade;
This only abides and glitters undecayed. 18

Seven grief's are as seven daggers in my heart,—
To see a lake without its lilied bloom,
The moon grow beggared of her radiant part,
Sweet woman's beauty fade towards the tomb,
A noble hug his wealth, a good man gone
Down in the press of miseries, a fair
And vacant face when knowledge is not there.
A base man standing by a monarch's throne. 55

Like shadows of the afternoon and morn
Friendship in good men is and in the base;
All vast the lewd man's in its first embrace,
But lessens and wears away; the other's, born
A dwarfish thing, grows giant-like apace. 59

Freely the sun gives all his beams to wake
The lotus slumbering in the darkened lake;
The moon unasked expends her gentle light,
Wooing to bloom her lily of the night;
Unasked the cloud its watery burden gives,
The noble nature in beneficence lives;
Unsought, unsued, not asking kindness back
Does good in secret for that good's sole sake. 73

Sri Aurobindo

❄❄❄❄❄

78
Verses on Love

When she lies on your chest
amid the disarray of her own scented hair,
with eyes like slightly opened buds
and cheeks flushed pink with love's fatigue,
the lips of a woman are honey
which favoured men drink. 123

When clouds shade the sky
and plantain lilies mask the earth,
when winds bear lingering scents
of fresh verbena and kadamba,
and forest retreats rejoice
to the cries of peacocks,
then ardent longing overpowers
loved and wretched men alike. 140

Renunciation of worldly attachment
is only the talk of scholars,
whose mouths are wordy with wisdom.
Who can really forsake the hips
of beautiful women bound
with girdles of ruby jewels? 147

Barbara Stoler Miller

In life this is the fruit of love:
two bodies with a single thought.
If, in the act of love, the mind
is elsewhere, it is like
the intercourse of corpses. 28

When minds are attuned
there is union
even in separation.
But if hearts are sundered,
even together,
people remain apart. 67

A scrawny cur,
one-eyed and lame,
with bitten ears
and tattered tail,
covered with sores
exuding pus
and full of maggots,
worn out, starving,
a broken potshead
round its neck:
and yet this dog
pursues the bitch.
Desire slayeth
even the slain. 80

A.N.D. Haksar

*****

79
Verses on Renunciation

For one short act, a child; next act, a boy
In love; then poor; a short act to enjoy
Status and wealth: till in the last act, Man,
Painted with wrinkles, body bent with age,
Ending the comedy which birth began,
Withdraws behind the curtain of life's stage. 235

She who is always in my thoughts prefers
Another man, and does not think of me.
Yet he seeks for another's love, not hers;
And some poor girl is grieving for my sake.
Why then, the devil take
Both her and him; and love; and her; and me. 311

Earth, my own mother; father Air; and Fire,
My friend; and Water, well-beloved cousin;
And Ether, brother mine: to all of you
This is my last farewell. I give you thanks
For all the benefits you have conferred
During my sojourn with you. Now my soul
Has won clear, certain knowledge, and returns
To the great absolute from whence it came. 301

John Brough

❄❄❄❄❄

DHARMAKĪRTI

From Subhāshita Ratnakosha

80
To ask no favours

To ask no favours from the wicked;
to beg not from a friend whose means are small;
to be in manner kindly and correct,
in conduct spotless even at the hour of death;
to keep one's stature in misfortune
and follow in the footsteps of the great:
in these rules, though hard to travel as a sword blade,
good men require no instruction. 1213

D.H.H. Ingalls

❄ ❄ ❄ ❄ ❄

81
Prestige

Vālmīki had the ocean bridged with mountains borne by monkeys;
And Vyāsa with Arjuna's arrows bridged the air;
still no one thinks this overdone.
Here I am, word and meaning balanced out,
yet people, wanting to fault
My verse, open their mouths wide.
Prestige, I bow low before you. 1726

V.N. Misra, L. Nathan and S. Vatsyayan

❄ ❄ ❄ ❄ ❄

82
The Lonely Path

No one behind, no one ahead.
The path the ancients cleared has closed.
And the other path, everyone's path,
easy and wide, goes nowhere.
I am alone and find my way. 1729

Octavio Paz

VIŚĀKHADATTA

Mudrarakshasa

83
Royal Power

Wary of too much attention, cold to the weak who can't hold her,
Scornful of fools, yet chary of those who know too much,
Fearful of courage, ready to mock the coward, the fortune
Of kings is hard to please as a whore when she's leading you on.

III. 5

V.N. Misra, L. Nathan and S. Vatsyayan

84
The Good Man

Does the tortoise feel no pain of weight
that he casts not Earth from off its back?
Or does the Illuminer of Day not tire
that he should never rest from motion?
Rather, a praiseworthy man would be ashamed
to give up meanly his appointed task.
The most sacred oath a good man keeps
is to fulfill his promise. II. 18

D.H.H. Ingalls

85
Autumn Skies

The skies, growing gradually peaceful,
flow like long rivers across heaven,
with sand banks formed of the white clouds
and scattered flights of softly crying cranes;
rivers which fill at night with waterlily stars. III. 7

D.H.H. Ingalls

❄ ❄ ❄ ❄ ❄

BĀṆA

Harshacharita

86
The Horse

The horse on rising stretches backward his hind legs,
lengthening his body by the lowering of his spine;
then curves his neck, head bending to his chest,
and shakes his dust-filled mane.
In his muzzle the nostrils quiver
in search of grass. He whinnies softly
as with his hoofs he paws the earth. III. 5

D.H.H. Ingalls

❄❄❄❄❄

From Subhāshita Ratnakosha

87
The Traveller at the Well

His gesture of cupped hands is from afar
and not for drinking water;
he shakes his head in wonder at her beauty,
not from slaking of his thirst;
the bristling of his flesh derives from pleasure,
not from water's coolness.
The traveller takes to strange behaviour
when he sees the girl who tends the well. 514

D.H.H. Ingalls

❄❄❄❄❄

88

Forest Fire

The puff of smoke from the forest fire,
black as the shoulder of a young buffalo,
curls slightly, spreads, is broken for a moment, falls;
then gathers its power gracefully, and rising thick,
it slowly lays upon the sky
its transient ornaments. 1174

D.H.H. Ingalls

❄❄❄❄❄

DIVAKARA

From Śārngadhara Paddhati

89

The Spread of Fame

What is the use of gossip about what goes on in other people's houses?
  But I am not able
to remain silent, with my naturally loquacious southern temperament:
In every house, in the markets, also in the square or at a drinking party,
Your beloved wanders about like a drunken woman—well! She is Fame!
1227

A.K. Warder

*****

AMARU

Amaruśataka

90
Love Poems

1

The day is surely better than the night?
Or is the night not better than the day?
How can I tell? But this I know is right:
Both are worth nothing when my love's away. 125

John Brough

2

When the pet parrot in the morning starts
To chatter rather much of what he heard
Of last night's talk between the young sweethearts,
The young wife does her best to check the bird,
Embarrassed that the older folk should hear,
And quickly stops his beak, trying to feed
The creature with a ruby from her ear,
Pretending it's a pomegranate seed. 16

John Brough

3

Well, but you surely do not mean to spend
Your whole life pining? Show some proper spirit.
Are there no other men? What is the merit
Of faithfulness to one? But when her friend
Gave this advice, she answered, pale with fear,
'Speak soft. My love lives in my heart, and he will hear.' 70

John Brough

4

He's stopped loving me
no longer cherished in his heart
no more affection for me
passes me in the street doesn't know me

O friend as I go on looking back
With longing for those lost days
What keeps my heart from falling to pieces? 43

W.S. Merwin and J.M. Masson

5

She let him in
She did not turn away from him
there was no anger in her words
She simply looked straight at him
as though there had never been
anything between them 114

W.S. Merwin and J.M. Masson

6

Held her
tight to me
breasts pressed flat
all of her skin
reached
and with wanting alone
her clothes by themselves fell down
her legs No
don't oh
god don't
too much oh
yes
she was saying I
could hardly hear her
after that did she
fall asleep did she die
did she vanish into me
did she totally dissolve
into me. 40

W.S. Merwin and J.M. Masson

7

To go
if you have really decided
then you will go
why hurry
two or three oh little white stay
while I look at
your face
living we are water running from
a bucket
who knows
whether I will see you
and you will see
me again 163

W.S. Merwin and J.M. Masson

8

How have you come to be
so thin
why are you trembling
why are you so
pale oh
simple girl
and she answered the lord of her life
all these things
just happen for no reason
sighing as she said it
and turning away to let
tears fall 50

W.S. Merwin and J.M. Masson

9

Let my eyes, trembling,
turn when seen by him;
let the poor girdle slip
and the bodice break from the heaving of my breast.
Still I shan't speak again
to my sweetheart who is false;
that is, unless my heart
should burst within me from my silence. 146

D.H.H. Ingalls

10

All night it rained,
the distant skies thundered
as he tossed and turned in his bed
and could not sleep. He sighed.
His eyes filled with tears
as he kept thinking of his young wife
lying alone in bed. He wept
aloud, he cried till daybreak came.
That was when the villagers decreed.
no traveller should be allowed
to stay back at night again. 13

Pritish Nandy

❄❄❄❄❄

DAṆḌIN

From Subhāshita Ratnakosha

91
Epigrams

This your coral nether lip
is like a desert path,
for whose heart, fair lass,
does it not make thirsty? 492

I've made no money,
gained no knowledge,
and won no merit.
And now my time is up. 1512

D.H.H. Ingalls

❄❄❄❄❄

KUMĀRADĀSA

Jānakiharaṇa

92

The Quarrel

In their quarrel she
pretended to be
asleep until he
shaking with passion
started to take off her dress
thief she said laughing and
boldly she bit
his lower lip VIII. 52

W.S. Merwin and J.M. Masson

* * * * *

From Subhāshita Ratnakosha

93

As the Wind Blows

As the wind blows, bearing drops of frost,
the god of love, as though he feared the cold,
hastily enters the hearts of lonely wives
to warm himself at the fire of their grief. 1137

D.H.H. Ingalls

* * * * *

BHAṬṬA NĀRĀYAṆA

Veṇīsamhāra

94
The Challenge

He who dragged the daughter of Pānchāla,
weeping, by the hair;
who tore away her robe
before the kings and elders;
he from whose breast I swore
to drink the blood like wine
has fallen in my hands, O Kauravas.
Come save him if you can. III. 47

D.H.H. Ingalls

* * * * *

95
Vengeance

Whoever, proud of his courage, carries arms in the Pandava troops,
Whoever belongs to the Pandava clan—child, adult, sleeper in the womb,
Whoever saw that act or meets me, front to front, in combat—
I'll kill then all in my fury, even kill the Great Killer, Himself. III. 32

V.N. Misra, L. Nathan and S. Vatsyayan

* * * * *

From Subhāshita Ratnakosha

96
True Strength

It is in rain, when mad, that you uproot the wayside tree;
and wherefore thrash the lake that blooms with lotuses?
O best of elephants, we shall admit your strength
when you touch the mane of a sleeping lion cub. 1072

D.H.H Ingalls

* * * * *

SANKARA

Saundaryalahari

97
In Praise of the Goddess

Slender as a streak of lightning,
composed of the essence of sun, moon and fire,
situated above the six lotuses, the manifestation
of you in the forest of great lotuses,
those with mind free of stain and illusion
who view it, mighty ones, experience a flood of supreme joy. 21

Let my idle chatter be the muttering of prayer,
my every manual movement the execution of ritual gesture,
my walking a ceremonial circumambulation,
my eating and other acts the rite of sacrifice,
my lying down prostration in worship,
my every pleasure enjoyed with dedication of myself,
let whatever activity is mine be some form of worship of you. 27

Bearing a mark of vermilion so that
the impenetrable darkness of your thick locks
with the hosts of their beauties
makes it seem like an imprisoned ray of the new-risen sun,
may it bring welfare to us, as though the flood of beauty
of your face had a channel to flow in,
the streak of which is the part in your hair. 44

Your right eye, because it has the sun as its essence,
  gives birth to the day;
Your left eye, which has the moon as its substance,
  produces the night;
Your third eye, which resembles a golden lotus
  slightly opened, creates the twilight
intervening between day and night. 48

W. Norman Brown

*****

Moha Mudgara

98
The Shattering of Illusion

Who is thy wife? Who is thy son?
The ways of this world are strange indeed.
Whose art thou? Whence art thou come?
Vast is thy ignorance, my beloved.
Therefore ponder these things and worship the Lord. 8

Behold the folly of Man:
In childhood busy with his toys,
In youth bewitched by love,
In age bowed down with cares—
And always unmindful of the Lord!
The hours fly, the seasons roll, life ebbs,
But the breeze of hope blows continually in his heart. 12

Birth brings death, death brings rebirth:
This evil needs no proof.
Where then, O Man, is thy happiness?
This life trembles in the balance
Like water on a lotus-leaf—
And yet the sage can show us, in an instant,
How to bridge this sea of change. 4

When the body is wrinkled, when the hair turns grey,
When the gums are toothless, and the old man's staff
Shakes like a reed beneath his weight.
The cup of his desire is still full. 15

Thy son may bring thee suffering,
Thy wealth is no assurance of heaven:
Therefore be not vain of thy wealth,

Or of thy family, or of thy youth—
All are fleeting, all must change.
Know this and be free.
Enter the joy of the Lord. 11

Seek neither peace nor strife
With kith or kin, with friend or foe.
O beloved, if thou wouldst attain freedom,
Be equal unto all. 25

Swami Prabhavananda and Christopher Isherwood

*****

YAŚOVARMAN

From Subhāshitāvali of Vallabhadeva

99

The Intolerance of Fate

The blue lotus which had charm similar to your eyes
  is sunk under the water,
The Moon which imitated the radiance of your face,
  beloved, is screened by the clouds,
Those white geese too, whose steps conformed to your walk,
  have gone;
My fate does not tolerate even the mere diversion
  of your likeness 1366

A. K. Warder

❄❄❄❄❄

SARAHA

Dohākośa

100
The Boatman

The body is the boat, the mind is at the helm,
Following the words of the good teacher, hold on, O boatman!

Refrain
Hey, boatman! Hold on with a firm mind,
There is no other means to reach the far side!

The boatman guides the boat with a rope;
Hold on and go naturally, not otherwise!

On the way there is danger to the boat, despite the heavenly bodies,
For everything sinks in the waves of transmigration.

Following the multitude it rises in the cutting stream:
Saraha says it attains the sky! 38. 1-4

A.K. Warder

❄❄❄❄❄

RAVIGUPTA

From Subhāshitāvali

101
Wickedness

A low person who gets promotion
first of all harms his master:
For on the road the powder of dust
first covers him who raises it. 414

Because of their natural villainy, even a good quality
in bad men oppresses people, like a fault;
the scent of poisonous flowers nauseates minds,
even when fragrant. 413

'His body is calm, there is no danger from him'—
this is not decisive:
Do not white wicks of lamps produce black soot? 2855

It does not exist, it does not exist for long, if it does
exist for long it is inconsistent with its result:
The anger of good men is similar to the affection
of the worthless. 236

A.K. Warder

*****

KOŪHALA

Lilāvai

102
A Mistress of Arts

In front of that palace we saw a girl sitting
on a delightful jewelled mosaic,
Like the fortune of the garden grove.

Engrossed in playing the *vinā* she turned her neck
so that she glanced upwards
And saw our flying chariot stopped in the skyway.

And she spoke, rising to greet us with words of sweet
syllables and not forgetting politeness,
Good nature in her heart and bowing with a salute:

"Ladies descend! Come and see this garden palace
like the Nandana grove,
It's beauty made a courtesy of lotus flowers in their own place."

When, sir, we had accepted comfortable seats, we asked
that young woman, "Charming one,
Tell us who you are.

Whose is this hand skilled in sketching various
beautiful things on a leaf?
And whose are these excellent *vinās* we see, with beautiful tones?

And whose are these palettes indicating
the entire collection of arts,
Their surface painted with beautiful mixings?

And whose, charming one, are these various weapons
We see, decorated with sandal paste?

And whose is this bookstand we see, slender one,
piled with books?
Tell us whose is this excellent palace, like
the abode of the Divine Architect?" 358-361, 363-367

A.K. Warder

GOVINDA

Svayambhuchanda

103
Cattle in the Moon Light

Remaining here and there at night
  having desisted from feeding,
Their cheeks moving as they chew the cud,
White and brilliant the herds of cattle are seen
  like treasures of moonlight 9.5

A.K. Warder

*****

BHAVABHŪTI

Uttara Rāma Charita

104
Deep in Love

Deep in love
cheek leaning on cheek we talked
of whatever came to our minds
just as it came
slowly oh
slowly
with our arms twined
tightly around us
and the hours passed and we
did not know it
still talking when
the night was gone I. 27

W.S. Merwin and J.M. Masson

❄❄❄❄❄

105
Great Hearts

Who can understand
the hearts of the truly great,
which are harder than diamonds
and softer than flowers? II. 7

D.H.H Ingalls

❄❄❄❄❄

106

Mountain River

These are the Southern Mountains, their
highest blue peaks supported by clouds,
With the gurgling roaring of the waters of the
Godāvari in their caverns;
These are the sacred confluences of rivers with
deep waters, wild
With the clamouring of turbulent waves
confused by repulsing one another. II. 30

A.K. Warder

❄❄❄❄❄

107

The Beloved

She is Heaven's blessing in my house,
She is a salve of nectar to my eyes.
Her cool hands when they touch my body
Refresh and comfort more than any liquid sandal.
Her arms around my neck are smooth as snow,
Lovely as pearl-lustre.
How can she ever bring me anything but happiness?
—Except for one thing.
How could I ever bear her loss? I. 38

John Brough

❄❄❄❄❄

108

Bitter Grief

Such bitter grief as this has cracked my heart,
Which still has not burst apart;
And from my body, fainting form the smart,
The senses do not depart.

Internal fires within my body blaze,
  And yet I am not consumed:
Fortune has cleft me with a mortal wound,
  Yet still I live out my days. III. 31

John Brough

✻✻✻✻✻

Mālati Mādhava

109
Her Glances

Her glances first came hesitant and sidelong,
then soft and shy with love;
a while they rested on me motionless,
then slowly turned away.
Her pupils widening behind long lashes
told of the admiration that she felt.
My heart, poor thing without defence, was captured
  cut up, swallowed,
and now is lost for aye. I. 31

D.H.H. Ingalls

✻✻✻✻✻

110
Medley of Emotions

Snatching my beloved out of range of the
  knife blow of this brigand, through fate,
observing her face grazed, like the crescent
  Moon by Rahu;
How does my heart endure, weak with terror,
  melting with compassion,
shaken with astonishment, blazing with anger,
  opening with joy? V. 28

A.K. Warder

111
The Proud Poet

Are there any around who mock my verses?
They ought to know I don't write for them.
Someone somewhere sometime will understand.
Time has no end. The world is big. I.6

V.N. Misra, L .Nathan and S. Vatsyayan

*****

VIDYĀ

From Subhāshita Ratnakosha

112
To the River Murala

Smooth banks of sand, thick shade of cane hungover the water,
The rustle of cooling winds, bearing delicious spray—
All supplies for endless good times for the brave at love—
Tell me, Murala, who dreamed up this marvelous notion? 809

V. N. Misra, L. Nathan and S. Vatsyayan

*****

113
To Her Friends

You are fortunate, dear friends, that you can tell
what happened with your lovers:
the jests and laughter, all the words and joys.
After my sweetheart
put his hand to the knot of my dress,
I swear that I can remember nothing. 574

D.H.H. Ingalls

*****

114
Jumna's Bank

Say, friend, if all is well still with the bowers
that grow upon the Jumna bank,
companions to the dalliance of cowherd girls
and witnesses of Radha's love.
Now that there is no use to cut their fronds
to make them into beds for love,
I fear their greenness will have faded
and they grown old and hard 808

D.H.H. Ingalls

From Saduktikarṇāmrita of Śridharadāsa

115
Love in the Countryside

Hiding in the
cucumber garden
simple country girl shivers
with desire
her lover on a low cot
lies tired with love
she melts into his body
with joy
his neck tight in her arms
one of her feet
flicking a necklace of
sea shells hanging
on a vine
on the fence
rattles them to scare off
foxes there in the dark II. 21.4

W.S. Merwin and J.M. Masson

* * * * *

DĀMODARAGUPTA

Kuṭṭanīmata

116
The Harlot's Experience

A stupid young brahman, not clever, cruel
in his exertions, for whom a woman is a rare thing,
Set about me in the night: sudden death
Pretending to be a lover. 392

Listen, friend, to the curious thing done today
by a rustic lover;
When I closed my eyes in the enjoyment of
love making, he said: 'She's dead!' and,
frightened, let me go! 398

A.K. Warder

❄ ❄ ❄ ❄ ❄

MURĀRI

Anargharāghava

117
The Lord of Lanka

Hearing that Daśaratha's sons were on the slope of Mount Suvela,
with half his twenty hands the king of Lanka gladly cleaned his sword,
and filled the four directions with the twanging of his bow;
but still the other ten were practicing their skill
in tracing on his painting board the tendril lines
of dark cosmetic worn by Sita on her breast. VI. 17

D.H.H. Ingalls

❄❄❄❄❄

118
In Praise of Vālmīki

These phrases of Murāri are like a trough beside a well;
the well: the nectar of Vālmīki's verse,
deep and delicious from its praise
of a dynasty so brilliant as was Rama's. I. 12

D.H.H. Ingalls

❄❄❄❄❄

119
The Courtier

Halting of voice and limb,
flattering the mighty,
I have been made an actor in a farce.
I know not what new comedy
old age will have me dance
with these white hairs for grease paint. III. 1

D.H.H Ingalls

120

The Moon Knows

The moon knows by how much her beauty fails,
Weighed against yours, to bring the balance even.
Look! In a vain attempt to turn the scales
she adds as makeweight all the stars of heaven. VII. 81

John Brough

❄ ❄ ❄ ❄ ❄

ŚĪLĀ BHAṬṬĀRIKĀ

From Subhāshita Ratnakosha

121
A Memory

My husband is the same who took my maidenhead
and these the moon-drenched nights we knew;
the very breeze is blowing from the Vindhya hills
heavy with scent of newly blossomed jasmine.
I too am still the same;
and yet with all my heart I yearn for the reed beds by the
stream
which knew our happy, graceful,
unending bouts of love. 815

D.H.H Ingalls

* * * * *

122
The Messenger

"You are panting!"
"I've been running."
"Your cheeks are flushed."
"You won. He lost."
"Your braid's loose."
"Because I fell at his feet."
"You look tired."
"The amount of talking I had to do!"
"Your dress knot's untied."
"Oh, I was careless."
"And what about your lips,
dear, lying messenger,
why do you think that they
look like two faded lotuses?" 850

P. Lal

* * * * *

ASAGA

Vardhamanācharita

123
Pen Pictures

In which in the evening the moonlight, white from the foam of ambrosia,
entering through a round window
Was tasted on the jewelled mosaic
by a delighted kitten desiring milk I. 35

In the summer when the woods are twisted by the flames of forest fires;
remaining on a mountain in the fierce rays of the sun,
His body dried up though his firmness does not waver for a moment
here;
The sage's endurance of heat proclaims his resignation. XV. 106

A.K. Warder

❄❄❄❄❄

VIKAṬANITAMBĀ

From Subhāshita Ratnakosha

124
Recollection

At the side of the bed
the knot came undone by itself,
and barely held by the sash
the robe slipped to my waist.
My friend, it's all I know: I was in his arms
and I can't remember who was who
or what we did or how 572

Octavio Paz

* * * * *

From Subhāshitāvali

125
The Advice

Don't worry about this young girl being very frail.
Have you ever seen a mango-blossom break from
 the weight of a bee?
You should squeeze her
When you are alone
Very hard.
And show no mercy.
Sugarcane softly pressed does not yield its full juice. 1401

V.S. Merwin and J.M. Masson

* * * * *

From Subhāshita Ratnakosha

126
River of Beauty

This woman is a strange river of beauty:
In her, lotuses sway to the moon,
And are those elephant heads submerged?
Banana stems lie by the lotus stalks. 426

V.N. Misra, L. Nathan and S. Vatsyayan

❄❄❄❄❄

VALLANA

From Subhāshita Ratnakosha

127
The Month of May

The month of May is sweet;
the forest lonely; you are young;
and I am well equipped
and of the age when love is strong.
So go your way, my sweet,
or stay with me a while.
The tattle-tales already have
The evidence they need. 1693

D.H.H. Ingalls

128
When he had taken off my clothes

When he had taken off my clothes,
unable to guard my bosom with my slender arms,
I clung to his very chest for garment.
But when his hand crept down below my hips,
What was to save me, sinking in a sea of shame,
If not the god of love, who teaches us to swoon? 568

D.H.H. Ingalls

129
Beauty

Beauty is not
in what the words say
but in that which they say without saying it:
not naked, but through a veil,
breasts become desirable. 1705

Octavio Paz

ABHINANDA

Rāmacharita

130
Hanuman leaps over the Ocean

The sun has been circled by his tail,
    the moon has been pierced by his crest,
the clouds have been tossed by his mane,
    the stars have been attacked by his teeth,
he has crossed the ocean just with a glance,
    with its bright loud-laughing waves,
he has traversed in all directions the cruel
    fire of the glory of the Lord of Lanka. XV. 64

A.K. Warder

* * * *

From Subhāshita Ratnakosha

131
Country Scene

The wagon track, marked with juice from the crushed cane,
    carries a flag of saffron-coloured dust;
a flock of parrots settles on the barley ears
already bowed with grain;
a school of minnows swims along the ditch
    from paddy field to tank
and on the river bank the good mud cools
    the herd boy from the sun. 282

D.H.H. Ingalls

* * * * *

132
Friendship

A friendship where one cannot act without restraint,
where one takes no joy in friendly banter
and where one friend must ever fear the other:
to such a friendship one should give wide berth. 1295

D.H.H. Ingalls

❄❄❄❄❄

NĀRĀYANA

Hitopadeśa

133
On Nobility

A life which is well known to be
Of learning, fame and bravery,
Though even of a moment's span,
It is truly lived by man.
For even crows can long survive
By eating scraps to stay alive. 2.43

'This is mine, and this is not,'—
Thus do the small-minded see.
The large-hearted have always thought
The world itself a family. 1.71

As clusters of wild flowers do,
The high-minded have but courses two:
To be borne on every brow,
Or perish on some unknown bough. 1.134

A.N.D. Haksar

*****

134
On Transience

From that very night, O King,
When in the womb one comes to stay,
A ceaseless journey will him bring
Nearer death each passing day. 4.86

Drifting on the sea's expanse,
As two logs will meet by chance,
And having met, will part perforce —
Such is creatures' intercourse. 4.74

Where did all the mighty go
With cavalcades of splendour rare?
Witness to their passing show
Even now this earth does bear. 4.69

A.N.D. Haksar

❄ ❄ ❄ ❄ ❄

135
On Friends

For eyes a salve of pleasure pure,
Ever delightful to the mind,
In joy and grief a partner sure,
Such a friend is hard to find.
Others one meets everywhere,
Fair-weather friends for money yearning.
For judging if they are sincere,
The touchstone is a crisis burning. 1.211

To you he speaks the loving word,
But stabs you when your back is turned:
Such a friend one must give up —
He's cream atop a poisoned cup. 1.78

A.N.D. Haksar

❄ ❄ ❄ ❄ ❄

136
On Governance

The greatest gains will not be won
By deeds of daring rashly done,
Nor by minds which continue
To ponder over what to do.
But success there is bound to be
In prudence joined to bravery. 3.116

One who even guards a cent
From ever being wrongly spent,
As if a horde of gold it were;
But will spending millions dare
When circumstances so demand,
And do it with an open hand —
The goddess of prosperity
Will never leave one such as he. 3.123

Power which is arbitrary
And that which law and scriptures guide,
To each other are contrary
And cannot in one place abide.
Where can one for instance see
A place both dark and light to be. 3.97

A.N.D. Haksar

❄❄❄❄❄

137
On Hunger

A woman will her child foresake
When hunger's pangs she can't evade,
As will the famished mother snake
Eat eggs that she herself has laid:
What sins will not the starving do?
Men grown gaunt turn pitiless too. 4.60

A.N.D. Haksar

❄❄❄❄❄

138
Reflections

Wealth not used for charity,
Or enjoyed as it should be;
Strength by which the enemy
Is not put into jeopardy;
Learning of the sacred writ
If one does not practice it;
And the self which can't control
Its senses and its passions' role:
What with these is there to do?
(They do not serve their purpose true) 2.9

Who, on attaining affluence,
Does not succumb to arrogance?
When given up to pleasures, who
Can to trouble bid adieu?
Who has never jilted been
By women on this earthly scene?
Who escapes death's fearful sting?
And who's the favourite of the king?
Which beggar ever gets respect?
Which man is there who can expect,
When fallen in a villain's snare,
To come out safe, without a care? 2.151

As objects on the hillside glow
By nearness to the rising sun,
The lowly glitter even so
With some good companion. Pr. 46

A.N.D. Haksar

❋ ❋ ❋ ❋ ❋

DĀMODARAMIŚRA

Hanumannāṭaka

139
The Moon Disguised

The moon disguised in the red garb
of the sun who had just set,
stealthily stretched forth his arm
to embrace the sun's dear lotus.
When the lotus recognized him by his chill
and turned her face away,
The moon's old love, the lily, laughed
and turned him pale with shame. II.6

D.H.H. Ingalls

*****

140
The Arrows of Love

All your five arrows
have sunk upto the feather in my heart
and there are burned together with my body
in the fire of separation.
Alas, poor Love, that being weaponless
you can no longer overcome the world;
See, only I shall suffer
while others live in joy. V.23

D.H.H. Ingalls

*****

RĀJAŚEKHARA

Viddhaśālabhanjikā

141
The Dancer

The damsel of arched eyebrows,
gracefully circling as she whirls the disk,
constructs three parasols:
with her skirt of southern silk,
with her beautiful pearl necklace,
and with her whirling braid of hair. II.9

Her jeweled anklets jingle sharply at each precious step,
the girdle chimes, the pearl necklaces fly high,
the rows of golden bracelets cry aloud:
the fair-browed maid by her dancing with the disk
has carried off my heart. II. 6

D.H.H. Ingalls

* * * * *

142
Growing Up

No longer do they leave their locks disheveled,
but study how to braid their hair;
they tend their teeth and knot their skirts,
grow fond of amorous practice with their brows;
the motions of their eyes become oblique;
their words acquire ambiguity:
each moment shows a progress in coquetry
as childhood slips to youth. II. 5

D.H.H. Ingalls

* * * * *

KSHEMĪŚVARA

Chaṇḍakauśika

143
The Sacrificial Tree

On the trunk of the Goddess's tree, where an imprint
has been made of five bloody fingers,
Where these crows cry out, eager for the offerings
of the common people;
After being shaken on the necks of dead buffaloes
and cattle, bells are hanging
With a shrill jangling pungent to the ears, with a wealth
of old remains of flower offerings. IV. 12

A.K. Warder

*****

SIDDHA

Upamitibhavaprapancha Kathā

144
The Beggar Unmeritorious

There was a certain starveling with a big belly,
named Unmeritorious,
Who had lost his relatives, was foolish, without
money or energy;
His body was weak with hunger: taking alms in
a broken pot
He wandered ceaselessly, wretched, blamed
at every house;
Without a protector and his sides and spine sore
from sleeping on the ground,
All his limbs grey with dust, garlanded with
a net-like rag,
Beaten at every moment by multitudes of
insolent children,
Injured by the blows of sticks, fists and great clods...

He was mad, had fever, leprosy, scabs, dysentery,
Was the hiding place of all diseases, delirious
in his agitation and pain.

He was seen by good men as a place for pity, he was
a cause of laughter to the proud,
A house of play for children, an example of bad actions.

If he got nothing at all he was only very distressed,
But getting a mere morsel of bad food contented him
as if it were a kingdom.

Chapter I

A.K. Warder

* * * * *

ANANTA

From Śārngadhara Paddhati

145
The Poet's Fame

People have passed, are passing, will pass
   On the earth, full of grief;
Fame belonging to literature
   Remains without loss. 150

A.K. Warder

* * * * *

KALAŚAKA

From Subhāshitāvali

146
Love Recalled

Her eyes half closed in drowsiness, languid
    with intoxication,
even now those sweet syllables of the deer-eyed one,
which are not meaningful, nor meaningless,
    how much they sound in my heart! 1280

A.K. Warder

*****

BHOJYA DEVA

From Subhāshita Ratnakosha

147
Apparition on the River Bank

She shakes her hair
and in the chaos of her curls
bright drops shine.
She crosses her arms and studies
the growing freshness of her breasts.
A cloth clings, translucid, to her thighs.
Bending slightly, with a quick glance
toward the bank, she comes out of the water. 1160

Octavio Paz

* * * * *

148
The Mango Grove

Many and many's the time in the mango grove
the hollow of my ear has drunk the cuckoo's song.
Today, though, as the sound approached
I shook in every limb.
My heart was sad, a trembling seized my eye,
Why thus, sweet friend, I prithee why? 350

D.H.H. Ingalls

* * * * *

ATULA

Mushikavaṃśa

149
A March through Kerala

The King saw bananas on the outskirts of Kolā
    with their leaves like hands waved in the wind
As if wishing to obtain some support
    when they were exhausted by their excessive loads of fruit.

The Lord of the Earth rejoiced abundantly in the villages
    at the scent of the splitting buds indicating the blossoms
Of groves of betel and forests of coconut,
    suddenly brought by the wind.

In the gaps in the fences whose colour was very dark
    with swarms of bees on the flowers of the creepers,
The faces of the women looking at the army
    attained the splendour of the moon observed in a gap in the clouds.

With their clusters of shaking flowers all round,
    the sugarcanes delighted the eyes of the armies,
Sporting hither and thither like rows
    of clumps of reeds of the chowrie bearers. II. 55-58

A.K. Warder

* * * * *

KSHEMENDRA

Kavikanṭhābharaṇa

150
The Poet

A poet should learn with his eyes
the form of leaves
he should know how to make
people laugh when they are together
he should get to see
what they are really like
he should know about oceans and mountains
in themselves
and the sun and the moon and the stars
his mind should enter into the seasons
he should go
among many people
in many places
and learn their languages. 10, 11

W.S. Merwin and J.M. Masson

*****

151
Punḍarīka

When he heard the news of his death
He stood without moving.
Then he let out a piteous cry
Loud enough to break the stones of the mountains,
Piercing his own life, rendering him unconscious:
O Punḍarīka!

Even now, long past, when the deer remember it
They drop the grass from their mouths. 25

W. S. Merwin and J. M. Masson

*****

SOMADEVA

Kathāsaritsāgara

152
The Merchant's Daughter

To the beat of the drum the thief was led
    to the place of execution,
and the merchant's daughter Ratnāvati
    sat on the terrace and watched him.
He was gravely wounded and covered with dust,
    but as soon as she saw him she was smitten with love.

Then she went to her father Ratnadatta, and said:
'This man they are leading to his death
    I have chosen for my lord!
Father, you must save him from the king,
    or I will die with him!'
And when he heard, her father said:
    'What is this you say, my child?
You've refused the finest suitors,
    the images of the Love-god!
How can you now desire
    a wretched master-thief?'

But though he reproached her thus
    she was firm in her resolve,
so he sped to the king and begged
    that the thief might be saved from the stake.
In return he offered
    the whole of his great fortune,
but the king would not yield the thief
    for ten million pieces of gold,
for he had robbed the whole city,
    and was brought to the stake to repay with his life.

Her father came home in despair,
    and the merchant's daughter
determined to follow
    the thief in his death.

Though her family tried to restrain her
    she bathed,
and mounted a litter, and went
    to the place of impalement,
while her father, her mother and her people
    followed her weeping.

The executioners placed
    the thief on the stake,
and, as his life ebbed away,
    he saw her come with her people.
He heard the onlookers speaking
    of all that had happened,
For a moment he wept, and then,
    smiling a little, he died.
At her order they lifted the corpse
    from the stake, and took it away,
and with it the worthy merchant's daughter
    mounted the pyre.

XII, 88.34-44

A.L. Basham

❄❄❄❄❄

BILHAṆA

Chaurapanchaśikā

153
Memories of Love

Even now
If my girl with lotus eyes came to me again
Weary with the dear weight of young love,
Again I would give to her these starved twins of arms
And from her mouth drink down the heavy wine,
As a reeling pirate bee in fluttered ease
Steals up the honey from the nenuphar. 3

E. Powys Mathers

Even now,
I remember her in love—
her body weak with fatigue
swarms of curling hair
falling on pale cheeks,
trying to hide
the secret of her guilt.
Her soft arms
clung
like vines on my neck. 4

Even now,
I remember her:
deep eyes' glittering pupils
dancing wildly in love's vigil,
a wild goose
in our lotus bed of passion—
her face bowed low with shame
at dawn. 5

Even now,
I remember the wine-smeared lips
she innocently licked in love,
her frail form, her wanton long eyes,
her body rubbed golden
with saffron paste and musk,
her mouth spiced
with camphor and betel-nut.

9

Barbara Stolen Miller

I still remember
and my heart aches.
It aches all day and night.
No, I will never see again
her beautiful, full moon face
aglow with a shine
that humbles
even the jasmine
that once tamed my night

32

Pritish Nandy

*****

DHANEŚVARA

Surasundari

154
When the Rains Came

One day when the new rains had thus arrived
King Suggīva, having ritually finished his meal,

His body smeared with sandalwood, putting on silk, soft,
smooth and spotless,
His hand busied with betel, went to the palace of the Queen.

He climbed to the topmost floor in the seven-storied palace;
The Queen politely seated him on a precious couch.

After passing a moment joking with his best beloved
He fell asleep on the soft mattress covered by a white sheet.

And then, his sleep destroyed by the thundering of the rain clouds,
He went out and sat on a cushion placed on a balcony.

Then Queen Kamalā too sat on half the King's seat.
Then the King spoke with a thrill, cheerful in the power of joy:

"At once the clouds (breasts) are delightful, sporting
strongly in meeting me;
Look, beloved, the North has become like you;

Look, slender one, the lightning displaying herself in the clouds,
Imitates the tremulousness of your eyes, the waviness of your hair.

Also, beloved, look, through the wandering Indra's herdsmen
The beauty of the rains is found fallen, powdered over the surface of the
earth."

At that time the Queen, being delighted, said to the King:
"O best of men, these rains have surpassed the rest of the seasons,

Since, having abandoned separated lovers, they are giving happiness to the labourers,
Calves, grass, herbs and so on as well as to the souls of lovers."

Then the King said, smiling a little: "O Queen, that is true:
A proverb has arisen which is heard here in the world:

Satisfied men earnestly see the circle of the directions as satisfied.
So, O Queen, being happy you think all are happy.

Yet all seasons, O Queen, are a cause of happiness for people with merit,
But for those without merit even the rains are a cause of unhappiness.

Or rather look, beautiful one, in a half-built, dilapidated hut,
Where a crowd of crying children is conspicuous in hundreds of pools of the floods;

Goaded excessively by his wife again and again, wretched,
His body without protection, struck by showers of water,

The hair bristling in his pores, his limbs shrinking in the cold wind,
That poor man with great difficulty repairs the hut.

Held by the ears, struck by heavy showers of water,
Observe a donkey in the corner of a roofless, broken temple."

II. 79-87, 94-102

A.K. Warder

*****

155
The Shipwreck

O King, as he thus told me his news,
The captain cried out thus in fear:

"Men of the crew, and coxswain, stand by!
There's a dreadful portent, like the face of Death, which

Has made a cloud the size of a winnowing basket into one
over the whole sky: look at the skyway,
As it makes a combination increasing at once, like a meeting of villains,

In a place like that a most horrible portent is produced:
Soon it causes destruction of ships, sailors with the stewards and the
rest."

Hearing such words from the man stationed at the top of the mast
support,
The crew were agitated, without hope of living.

Then:

The multitude of anchors was let go, the mast support was put flat
And the ship was all covered with the mass of white sails.

Meanwhile the sky was covered with a multitude of black clouds,
A fierce wind blew, making the sea agitated;

All round, a continual streaking of lightning amazes like
the tongue of Death
And the clouds thunder terrifyingly like Death's soldiers.

The ship was carried away by the impulses of the waves of the ocean
thrown up by the rough wind,
Though held by the multitude of anchors which rose through the power
of heavy billows;

She drifts making play, rising and falling, of being struck seductively
By rubbing hands, through the incessant waves.

And now in a moment whipped by the churning of the rough wind
The anchors broke with a crack under the impulses of the waves.

The ship let loose from its bonds by them, like an excellent filly,
Ran impelled by the heavy impulses of the waves;

Now flying up in the sky like a wizard woman who has mastered the
sciences,
Now falling down from the sky like a wizard woman losing her sciences;

Now like a female snake struck with a stick she goes waving to and fro,
Now like a woman very frightened by a crowd she runs very fast.

Through the lamentation of the loud noise emitted by all the planks as their bonds separated,
She wailed as if afraid of imminent wrecking, deprived of a refuge;

As if mad then whirling hither and thither in the ocean,
Incessantly splitting like an unbaked dish in the water;

Her coxswain exceeded, the crowd of hands confused and babbling,
Her caravan of merchants frightened, the servants crying out loudly:

As the crowd of people was hiding pieces of gold in their loincloths and lips,
The multitude of merchants was skilled in garlanding their bodies with pieces of plank,

All the people were beseeching the multitude of their family deities
And the crew were throwing the cargo into the sea,

The ship was attacked by a mountainous mace bordered with a guise of water
And suddenly burst into a multitude of splitting planks.

XII. 188-201, 205-210

A.K. Warder

*****

JAYADEVA

Gītagovinda

156

Song in the Melody Gurjari

Sweet notes from his alluring flute echo nectar from his lips.
His restless eyes glance, his head sways, earrings play at his cheeks.
My hearts recalls Hari here in his love dance,
Playing seductively, laughing, mocking me.

A circle of peacock plumes caressed by moonlight crowns his hair.
A rainbow colours the fine cloth on his cloud-dark body.
My heart recalls Hari here in his love dance,
Playing seductively, laughing, mocking me.

Kissing mouths of round-hipped cowherd girls whets his lust.
Brilliant smiles flash from the ruby-red buds of his sweet lips.
My heart recalls Hari here in his love dance,
Playing seductively, laughing, mocking me.

Vines of his great throbbing arms circle a thousand cowherdesses.
Jewel rays from his hands and feet and chest break the dark light.
My heart recalls Hari here in his love dance,
Playing seductively, laughing, mocking me.

His sandalpaste browmark outshines the moon in a mass of clouds.
His cruel heart is a hard door bruising circles of swelling breasts.
My heart recalls Hari here in his love dance,
Playing seductively, laughing, mocking me.

Jeweled earrings in sea-serpent form adorn his sublime cheeks.
His trailing yellow cloth is a retinue of sages, gods, and spirits.
My heart recalls Hari here in his love dance,
Playing seductively, laughing, mocking me.

Meeting me under a flowering tree, he calms my fear of dark time,
Delighting me deeply by quickly glancing looks at my heart.
My heart recalls Hari here in his love dance,
Playing seductively, laughing, mocking me. II. 2-8

Barbara Stoler Miller

157
Song in the Melody Rāmakari

Sandal and garment of yellow and lotus garlands upon
his body of blue,
In his dance the jewels of his ears in movement dangling over
his smiling cheeks.
Hari here disports himself with charming women given to love!

The wife of a certain herdsman sings as Hari sounds a tune of love
Embracing him the while with all the force of her full and swelling
breasts.
Hari here disports himself with charming women given to love!

Another artless woman looks with ardour on Krishna's lotus face
Where passion arose through restless motion of playful eyes
with sidelong glances.
Hari here disports himself with charming women given to love!

Another comes with beautiful hips, making as if to whisper a word,
And drawing close to his ear the adorable Krishna she kisses upon the
cheek.
Hari here disports himself with charming women given to love!

Another on the bank of the Jamna, when Krishna goes to a bamboo
thicket,
Pulls at his garment to draw him back, so eager is she for amorous play.
Hari here disports himself with charming women given to love!

Hari praises another woman, lost with him in the dance of love,
The dance where the sweet low flute is heard in the clamour
of bangles on hands that clap.
Hari here disports himself with charming women given to love!

He embraces one woman, he kisses another, and fondles
another beautiful one,
He looks at another one lovely with smiles, and starts in
pursuit of another woman.
Hari here disports himself with charming women given to love!

May all prosperity spread from this, Shri Jayadeva's
famed and delightful
Song of wonderful Keshava's secret play in the forest of Vrindāvana!
Hari here disports himself with charming women given to love! I. 38-45

George Keyt

*****

158
Song in the Melody Vasanta

In spring when tender Malayan breezes fondle the
beautiful creepers of clove,
And huts and bowers resound with the mingled noise
of bees and kokilā birds,

Hari here in the forest dwells, in eager dance with the
women folk—
It is hard to endure being parted in spring, my friend!

In spring when the violent odour of musk is the scent of
the tender tamāla sprout,
When the colour of kimsuka flowers, the nails of the
love god's fingers, tears young hearts,

Hari here in the forest dwells, in eager dance with the
women folk—
It is hard to endure being parted in spring, my friend!

In spring when the love lord's golden staff is seen in the colour of
keshara flowers,
When bees which come to the clustering pātala make that flower the
quiver of love,

Hari here in the forest dwells, in eager dance with the
women folk—
It is hard to endure being parted in spring, my friend!

In spring when the blossoming mangoes thrill to the clasp
of the tremulous vernal creepers,
When the Vrindāvan forest is cleansed by the water of Jamna
meandering through the wood,

Hari here in the forest dwells, in eager dance with the
women folk—
It is hard to endure being parted in spring, my friend!

This, the description—the forest in springtime, delightful—
threaded with phases of passion,
The purpose of which is to recollect Hari, wells up in the
utterance of Shri Jayadeva.

Hari here in the forest dwells, in eager dance with the
women folk—
It is hard to endure being parted in spring, my friend!

I.27, 29-30, 33-34

George Keyt

*****

HARIBHAṬṬA

From Subhāshitāvali

159
The Wise and the Great

A wise man who has a mind to obtain a desired result,
whether small or great,
should not remain inactive even for a moment:
For, if the potter does not ceaselessly whirl the wheel
with his stick,
though the clay is there, there is no dish nor water jar. 2936

Delight in things well said, no exaltation in fortune;
action more able in producing for others;
Insatiability with good qualities and respect for those
possessing them:
this is the hidden life of the great. 269

A.K. Warder

❄❄❄❄❄

MANOVINODA

From Subhāshita Ratnakosha

160
Birds

The kite looking below turns his head obliquely
on either side,
Slowly glides in a delicate circle in the sky
on his wings immobile;
Subtle in feeding, after a long time, falling sidelong
most swiftly,
Unexpectedly he hurls himself with trembling
feet and head. 273

The wagtail acts a little while near his beloved
whose glance rests keen, her eyes motionless
in the waves of tears of joy;
His tail lifted high, legs in tempo, wings quivering low,
beak slightly loquacious with the sweet notes
of intoxication high in his throat. 274

A.K. Warder

*****

NAYACHANDRA SURI

Hammīra Mahākāvya

161
The Dancer on the Rampart

In time the drummers beat their drums, the lutanists plucked their
lutes,
the flautists blew their flutes.
Their voices in tune with the shrill flutes, the singers
sang the glory and fame of the brave Hammīra...
Then, the vine of her body entrancing her lovers,
awakening passion with the glance of her half-closed eyes,
to delight the hearts of the courtiers,
came Rādhādevī the dancer, arrayed for the dance.

The quivering buds of her fingers moved in the dance
like tendrils of a vine, thrilling with passion. ...
As the tips of her fingers bent, as though in a circle,
with her grace and delicate beauty all other girls seemed her slaves.
The moon, in the guise of the ring that trembled from the tip of her ear,
said: 'Your face is my likeness, the delusion even of sages!'
And as she danced she stirred the hearts of the young men watching—
the hearts which lay like motes of camphor under her feet...
With her gestures the necklace trembled on the tips of her breasts
like a lotus twined in the beak of a swan.
When her body bent back like a bow in the dance
like a bowstring the braid of her hair stretched down to her heel....

And as she danced, at every beat of the rhythm,
she turned her back on the Śaka king below.

Then in fury of soul the Lord of the Śakas spoke to his chamberlain:
'Is there any bowman who can make her his mark?'
His brother said: 'Sire, there is he whom you formerly threw into prison,
Uḍḍānasiṃha—he is the only man who can do it !'
At once the Śaka king had him brought, and struck off his fetters,

and arrayed the traitor finely, with double gift of affection.
And thus apparelled he took the bow which none but he could draw,
and the sinner shot her, as a hunter shoots a doe.

At the stroke of the arrow she fainted and fell in the moat,
as lightning falls from heaven."

XII. 13-32

A.L. Basham

* * * * *

RŪPA GOSVĀMIN

Ujjvalanīlamaṇi

162
The Cowherd's Daughter

Oh friend you
play in the mud like a child
your blouse not
even covering your breasts
your father the cowherd
thinking you still a child
has done nothing
to find you a husband
but then suddenly
your eyelids leap us as you hear
in the Vrindā forest the sound
of Krishna's flute
and you tremble with longing
and show the whites of your eyes 35

W.S. Merwin and J.M. Masson

* * * * *

163
In Love

That modesty
the weight of it
that I feel before my parents
I did away with
hoping to be happy with him
oh friend
oh friend all of you dearer
even than my own breathing
you were put to so much trouble so often
I paid no attention to
the holy laws taught to me

by chaste women
damn my obstinacy
wicked as I am
I go on living
though he pays no attention p. 342

W.S. Merwin and J.M. Masson

❄❄❄❄❄

JAGANNĀTHA

Rasagangādhara

164
The Retort

"Small-waisted girl why are you so thin?"
"Why do you concern yourself with other people's affairs?"
"Tell me nonetheless, and give me joy."
"Go away, traveller, your wife will tell you."

J. M. Masson

*****

Bhāminī Vilāsa

165
A Word of Warning

My soul, I tell you, watch out. Don't take up with
that cowherd.
Whose skin is the hue of fresh rain clouds, the one who
pastures
His herd in Vrindavana. He's shrewd. He'll charm you
first with his smile,
Then his looks. Your senses will fail, and then oblivion. 4.16

V.N. Misra, L. Nathan and S. Vatsyayan

*****

NĪLAKAṆṬHA DĪKSHITA

Kaliviḍambana

166
Satire on Physicians

There is no use of people in health and people with incurable diseases; the timid as well as those with prolonged ailments are the good fortune of doctors.

Neither too much courage nor too much fear should be instilled in the patient; in the former case, being rid of anxiety, he will not pay; and in the latter too, because of loss of hope, he will not pay.

Let the medical prescription be whatever it is; the diet restrictions should be severe; if he comes back to health, it is then due to the greatness of the doctors; if it is otherwise, it should be blamed on the violation of the diet-regulations.

As ailments spread and people die, doctors slowly educate themselves in the nature of diseases. 23-25, 27

V. Raghavan

* * * * *

ANONYMOUS VERSES FROM ANTHOLOGIES

From Subhāshitāvali of Vallabhadeva

167
Do not go

'Do not go,' I could say; but this is inauspicious.
'All right, go' is a loveless thing to say.
'Stay with me' is imperious. 'Do as you wish' suggests
Cold indifference. And if I say 'I'll die
When you are gone,' you might or might not believe me.
Teach me, my husband, what I ought to say
When you go away. 1049

John Brough

*****

168
My Love

Although I conquer all the earth,
Yet for me there is only one city.
In that city there is for me only one house;
And in that house, one room only;
And in that room a bed.
And one woman sleeps there,
The shining joy and jewel of all my kingdom. 1476

John Brough

*****

169
Love all you can

Love all you can,
Handsome young man.
Day after day
Youth steals away.
While you still live,
Why should you give
Death, for his share,
Something so fair? 2366

John Brough

❄❄❄❄❄

From Paddhati of Śārngadhara

170
Gentle Deer

Peaceful, the gentle deer untroubled graze:
All that they need, their forest-home supplies.
No greed for wealth nor envy clouds their days.
But these are only beasts, and we are wise. 261

John Brough

❄❄❄❄❄

171
The Burglar

'Give me that bit of rag; or take the boy
And try to keep him warm.' 'The ground this side
Is bare, and there's at least some straw at yours.'
The burglar who had quietly entered heard,
Threw over them the ragged clock he'd lifted
Elsewhere, and crept away again, in tears. 409

John Brough

172
The Compliment

Bee, you fly so far around:
Tell me, have you ever found,
Seen, or ever heard men tell
Of a flower to match the grace
— Speak, and do not fear to tell –
Of the gentle lily's face ? 818

John Brough

*****

173
A Marvel

O Poverty
great powers
you have given me
I see
the whole world
and nobody sees me. 402

W.S. Merwin and J.M. Masson

*****

174
The Teacher

I wear no bracelets
golden as the autumn moon;
I've never known the taste of the lips
of a timid and tender young girl;
I have never won, by sword or pen,
fame in the halls of time:
I wasted my life in broken-down colleges,
teaching insolent, malicious boys. 1469

Octavio Paz

175
The Invitation

Traveler, hurry your steps, be on your way:
the woods are full of wild animals,
snakes, elephants, tigers, and boars,
the sun's going down and you're so young to be going
 alone.
I can't let you stay,
for I'm a young girl and no one's home. 810

Octavio Paz

176
Rain in the Forest

Water pouring from the clouds
in the night
of palm forests
large ears motionless
they listen
the elephants
eyes half closed
to the sound of the heavy rain
their trunks resting on their tusks 1161

W.S. Merwin and J.M. Masson

177
A Come-hither Glance

Her hand upon her hip she placed,
And swayed seductively her waist;
With chin upon her shoulder pressed,
She stretched herself to show her breast:
With sapphire pupils burning bright
Within the pearly orbs of white,
Her eyes with eagerness did dance,
And threw me a come-hither glance. 465

John Brough

OTHER ANONYMOUS VERSES

Śuka Saptati

178
Springtime in the Forest

The forest smiles, the buds are gleaming,
it shines with mango blossoms teeming.
Here rows of milk trees, branches bent
with loads of fruit, so succulent;
there rose apple and timburini
in splendid clusters one may see.
Here serried oleanders shine,
there camphor spreads its fragrance fine.
Here jasmine fair and pepper vine
there mango, sandalwood and pine,
Champak, bakula, pomegranate flowers,
palms and jujube trees in bowers
by nets of climbing gourd entwined
so thick— the sky one cannot find.
The fruit is red on the karna plant,
others the jungle white rose flaunt;
some are covered by the wild anise,
and flowers bloom on sindur trees
in festoons which entrance the mind
with their glory incarnadined.
In blossom too are coral trees,
high acacias scent the breeze;
and other plants with blooms are dense,
double jasmine charms the sense. 41.196-207

A.N.D. Haksar

*****

Simhāsana Dvāṭriṃśikā

179
Gnomic Verses

Thirsty peacocks cry out in distress
to the rain clouds, and the clouds
instantly pour down streams of water for them.
What is the cloud to the bird,
or the bird to the cloud? Those who
are in distress should not
fail to ask, and those who are
great-hearted should not fail to give. VI.7

Even though they may endure for long,
sensual pleasures must inevitably fade away.
What difference does it make if people
will not give them up willingly?
If they cease on their own it grieves the heart
immeasurably; but if they are renounced,
it gives one the infinite happiness of peace. XVI.3

A.N.D. Haksar

❄❄❄❄❄

A SEASONAL ANTHOLOGY

From Subhāshita Ratnakosha of Vidyākara

180
The Six Seasons

Spring: Sāvarṇi
Bright chains of amaranth about their hips,
fresh mango blossoms at their ears,
the red *aśoka* on their breasts
and *mādhavi* within their hair,
their bodies rouged all over
with yellow pollen of the *bakula*:
Such is our lasses' costume; may its advent
bring joy to lusty lads. 177

Summer: Yogeśvara
The water of the pond is hot above
but sharply cold beneath.
When wayside wells run dry the travellers come at noon,
and, covered though it is with floating moss
and muddy from the wallowing of buffaloes
not yet harnessed to the plough,
they stir it with their arms and drink. 206

Rains: Bhavabhūti
Now come the days of changing beauty,
of summer's parting as the monsoon comes,
when the eastern gales come driving in,
perfumed with blossoming *arjuna* and sal trees,
tossing the clouds as smooth and dark as sapphires:
days that are sweet with the smell of rain-soaked earth. 218

Autumn: Viśākhadatta
The skies, growing gradually peaceful,
flow like long rivers across heaven,
with sand banks formed of the white clouds
and scattered flights of softly crying cranes;
rivers which fill at night with water-lily stars. 278

Early Winter: Abhinanda

The round villages are charming now at day's end
with threshing circles scattered on the common
for treading of the heaped up rice;
the dung fires cast a ring of smoke
that hangs low overhead from weight of frost. 303

Later Winter: Anon.

The heavy snow is falling, not easy to distinguish
among the smoke-grey *damanaka* trees,
but for the fire of dung it forms a tent of beauty.
At dawn it hides the rising sun,
and clinging to the travellers' furs,
shows them all white of every limb. 307

D.H.H. Ingalls

❄ ❄ ❄ ❄ ❄

POETRY FROM INSCRIPTIONS

The Mandasor Epigraph (436 CE)

181
The Weavers of Lāta

.... In the land of Lāta, the trees bend
under the weight of their flowers,
there are beautiful temples, royal halls, holy monasteries.
But the world-famous craftsmen of Lāta
left that land of theirs and its wooded mountains,

attracted by the good king of this region.
Despite the hardships of the journey,
they came with great hopes to Daśapura— at first
only in their daydreams, and then with children and kin...

They formed close associations
with their neighbors; day by day friendship grew.
The kings treated them like their own sons,
and they lived happily in Daśapura.

A girl can be very young and pretty,
gold at her neck, flowers in her hair and betel
in her mouth—yet the real beauty only comes
when she puts on her pair of silks.

And who makes the silk that adorns
the land far and wide— soft silk,
with a riot of colours, a true delight to see?
These craftsmen from Lāta.

Yet knowing that the life of man, and wealth,
however vast, are far more fragile
than a petal blown from the ear of a forest spirit,
they made a firm and good decision,

while King Kumaragupta was ruling the earth,
...

and Bandhuvarman was the lord
protecting the rich town of Daśapura:

With the wealth acquired from their craft
the guild of silk-weavers would have a temple built
a noble temple like no other, in honour of the blazing sun.
In the year four hundred ninety three
from the founding of the Mālava tribe,
during the time of year
when clouds begin to rumble
in the month of Sahasya, in the white fortnight,
the lucky thirteenth day, this place was opened, with hymns of praise.

As long as Lord Śiva bears his high pile
of matted yellow hair and pure crescent moon within;
as long as the bright lotus garland hangs
at Vishnu's shoulder, this noble house will last.

By order of the guild and with true devotion
this house of the sun was built;
and with great care the above was composed
by Vatsabhaṭṭi.

Sheldon Pollock

❄❄❄❄❄

The Changu Narayan Pillar, Nepal (464 CE)

182
The Queen and the Prince

His wife was the grand Śrī Rājyavatī.
She was the offspring of a pure family, a Lakshmī
to his Vishnu with all her virtues. And he loved her
more than life itself.

<... > the king had shed the lustre of his fame
over this whole world, but then he left
for the realm of the gods— it was peaceful, like a trip
to a pleasure garden— but his wife suddenly collapsed,

wild with the fever of grief <...> utterly immobilized—
a woman who before separation from her husband
was ever busy with rites and rituals and the feeding of the gods.
Now this Queen Rājyavatī— called the king's wife
but really his royal power incarnate—
was about to follow her husband,
her thoughts fixed on the other world.
She came to her son, Prince Mānadeva, a man
of faultless conduct, in beauty like the autumn moon
and like the moon a delight to all the people.
The words catching in her throat, drawing sighs
so slowly, her face stained with tears, she said,
with deep emotion, "Your father has gone to heaven.
O my son, there is no reason for me to live
now that your father has passed away. My dear son,
rule the kingdom, I will take the path
my husband took, before the day is out.

"How could I live without my husband, held back by the hope—
which long years of mutual pleasure still arouse—
of being reunited with him, when that could never be
more than a dream or mirage? I am going," she said
with determination. But then her broken-hearted son
touched his head to her feet in devotion and firmly spoke.

"What use would I have for pleasures, what possible joy
in living if I were parted from you?
First I will give up my life— and only then
can you go from this world to heaven." These words of his,
moistened with tears from his lotus eyes, were the cords
of a net that trapped her like a bird. And trapped she stayed...

Sheldon Pollock

* * * * *

The Merbabu Rock Inscription, Java
(C.7th Century CE)

183
The Spring

Her younger sisters are the pure white lotuses,
she gushes from the rock face here
and from among the pebbles there, and there
pours out her cold clean water,
this spring that like the Ganga makes all it touches pure.

Sheldon Pollock

*****

The Progress of Translation

Translations from Sanskrit into English over the years have reflected both the scholarship and the sensibilities of individual translators as well as the prevalent level of Sanskrit studies and the then ambience of English usage. This progression is illustrated here by bringing together some well known translations of the same text, also indicating their years of publication. Details of the translators are given in a separate list.

The texts selected as samples are celebrated verses from the dialogue of Kālidāsa's famous play *Abhijnānaśākuntala*, originally translated into English by the polymath Sir William Jones. The first is Act II, verse 11, in which the hero, King Dushyanta, describes his first encounter with Shakuntala, a girl from a hermitage, with whom he has fallen in love.

> .....yet she did look at me, wishing to be unperceived; then she smiled, and started a new subject of conversation. Love is by nature averse to a sudden communication, and hitherto neither fully displays, nor wholly conceals, himself in her demeanour towards me. *William Jones, 1789*

> She did look towards me, though she quick withdrew
> Her stealthy glances when she met my gaze;
> She smiled upon me sweetly, but disguised
> With maiden grace the secret of her smiles.
> Coy love was half unveiled; then, sudden checked
> By modesty, left half to be divined.
>
> *Monier Williams, 1856*

> When I was with her, her glance was still circumspect,
> Though she would smile when I spoke of external things;

Modest her bearings: her love was not yet revealed,
Nor was it quite concealed.

John Brough, 1965

Her eyes were caste down in my presence,
but she found an excuse to smile –
modesty barely contained the love
she could neither reveal nor conceal.

Barbara Stoler Miller, 1984

The second sample is Act IV, verse 6, acclaimed by ancient Indian critics as a classic. In it Shakuntala's foster-father, the hermit Kanva, is saddened at her departure from the hermitage to join Dushyanta in his capital.

> This day must Shakuntala depart: that is resolved; yet my soul is smitten with anguish. My speech is interrupted by a torrent of tears, which my reason suppresses and turns inward; my very sight is dimmed, — Strange that the affliction of a forester, retired from haunts of men, should be so excessive! – Oh! with what pangs must they, who are fathers of families, be afflicted on the departure of a daughter!

William Jones, 1789

This day my loved one leaves me, and my heart
Is heavy with its grief; the streams of sorrow
Choked at the source, repress my faltering voice,
I have no words to speak; mine eyes are dimmed
By the dark shadows of the thoughts that rise
Within my soul. If such the force of grief
In an old hermit parted from his nurseling,
What anguish must the stricken parents feel –
Bereft forever of an only daughter?

Monier Williams, 1856

Shakuntala must go today;
  I miss her now at heart;
I dare not speak a loving word
  Or choking tears will start.

My eyes are dim with anxious thought;
  Love strikes me to the life:
And yet I strove for pious peace –
  I have no child, no wife.
What must a father feel, when come
  The pangs of parting from his child at home?

Arthur W. Ryder, 1912

My heart is touched with sadness
since Shakuntala must go today,
my throat is choked with sobs,
my eyes are dulled with worry –
if a disciplined ascetic
suffers so deeply from love,
how do fathers bear the pain
of each daughter's parting?

Barbara Stoler Miller, 1984

The final example is Act V, verse 2, in which Dushyanta, who has forgotten Shakuntala, is struck by a subliminal memory as he hears another woman singing in the palace.

> Perhaps the sadness of men, otherwise happy, on seeing beautiful forms and listening to sweet melody, arises from some faint remembrance of past joys and the traces of connections in a former state of existence.

William Jones, 1789

Not seldom in our happy hours of ease,
When thought is still, the sight of some fair form,
Or mournful fall of music breathing low,
Will stir strange fancies, thrilling all the soul
With a mysterious sadness, and a sense
Of vague yet earnest longing. Can it be
That the dim memory of events long past,
Or friendships formed in other states of being,
Flits like a passing shadow o'er the spirit?

Monier Williams, 1856

Though you're contented now, some lovely thing,
The half-heard sound
Of words in a song can conjure a desire from nowhere
That your mind can't grasp, because the life before is crying
To the present life what it has loved, but cries from very deep

V.N. Misra, L. Nathan and S. Vatsyayan, 1983

Seeing rare beauty,
hearing lovely sounds,
even a happy man
become strangely uneasy….
perhaps he remembers,
without knowing why,
loves of another life
buried deep in his being.

Barbara Stoler Miller, 1984

The Poets

Abhinanda	Ninth century CE Pāla court poet. Author of the epic poem *Rāmacharita.*
Amaru	Reputed author of *Amruśataka*, the celebrated collection of love poems dated to about the 7th century CE.
Ananta	A king in 10th century CE Kashmir.
Asaga	Digambara Jaina monk from 9th century CE Karnataka. Author of the epic *Vardhamāna Charita.*
Aśvaghosha	Major Buddhist philosopher and writer, dated to the 1st century CE. His most famous work is the biographical poem *Buddhacharita.*
Atula	Author of the epic dynastic history *Mushikavamśa* from 11th century CE Kerala.
Bāṇa	Court poet of the 7th century CE King Harsha of Kannauj. His biographical work *Harshacharita* and romance *Kādambarí* established him as the leading prose stylist of Sanskrit.
Bhāravi	Author of the epic *Kirātārjunīya* which is dated to the 6th century CE during the Pallava empire. Acclaimed by later critics and cited along with Kālidāsa in the 634 CE Aihole inscription.
Bhartrihari	Reputed author of the well known *Śatakatrayam*, the three centuries of verse epigrams on life, love and renunciation. Sometimes identified with the distinguished 6th-7th century CE grammarian of the same name.
Bhāsa	Dramatist praised by celebrated later writers including Kālidāsa and Bāṇa. Dated usually to the 1st-2nd century CE. *Svapnavāsavadattā* is the best known of the plays ascribed to him.
Bhaṭṭa Nārāyaṇa	Author of the acclaimed 7th century CE play *Veṇīsamhara* about the Mahābhārata war.
Bhavabhūti	A major Sanskrit dramatist and poet, usually placed in 8th century CE central India. His best known plays are *Uttara Rāma Charita* and *Mālatimādhava.*

Bhojya Deva	Identified with the 11th century CE king Bhoja of Dhara, who was well known as a patron of poets and a writer on poetics himself.
Bilhaṇa	Poet from 11th-12th century CE Kashmir, author of *Vikramānkadevacharita,* about the deeds of a Karnataka ruler, and a collection of love poems, *Chaurapanchaśikā.*
Daṇḍin	Well known critic and prose stylist, placed in 7th century CE Kānchipuram during the Pallava empire. Author of *Kāvyādarśa*, a major work on poetics, and the prose romance *Dāśa Kumāra Charitam.*
Dāmodaragupta	Minister of the 8th century CE king Jayāpida of Kashmir, and author of *Kuṭṭanimata* a verse novel about the lives of courtesans.
Dāmodaramiśra	Reputed author of the 10th century CE play *Hanumannāṭaka* on the deeds of Rāma.
Dhaneśvara	Author of the Prakrit verse novel *Surasundari* probably from 11th century CE Rajasthan.
Dharmakīrti	Celebrated Buddhist philosopher and logician dated to the 7th century CE.
Divākara	A noted poet at the court of King Harsha of 7th Century CE Kannauj.
Govinda	Writer from c. 8th century CE, whose Apabhramśa verses are quoted in the collection *Svayambhuchandas.*
Hāla	Sātavahāna dynasty king in the 1st-2nd century CE. Traditionally regarded as the composer of the *Gāthā Sattasai*, an anthology of Prakrit verses on everyday life and love, whose individual authors are unspecified.
Haribhaṭṭa	Buddhist monk and writer dated to 12th century CE Kashmir.
Jagannātha	Poet and scholar associated with the court of the 17th century Mughal emperor Shahjehan. Author of the poetical works *Bhāminī Vilāsa* and *Rasagangādhara,* among others.
Jayadeva	Author of the famous *Gita Govinda,* a work of devotional lyrical poetry from 12th century eastern India.
Kalaśaka	A king in 10-11th century CE Kashmir.

Kālidāsa	Widely considered the outstanding poet and dramatist of classical Sanskrit. Usually placed at the Gupta imperial court in the 5th century CE, though there are several other opinions about his date and provenance.
Kouhala	Or Kutuhala. Probable author of the 8th century CE Prakrit verse novel *Līlavaī* or *Līlavatī.*
Kshemendra	Poet, polymath and prolific author from 11th century CE Kashmir.
Kshemiśvara	Author of the plays *Chanḍakauśika* and *Naishadhānanda*, probably during the 10-11th century Gurjara-Pratihāra king Mahipāla's reign in west-central India.
Kumāradāsa	Author of the 7th century CE epic poem *Jánakiharaṇa*, which was lauded by later critics like Rājasekhara.
Māgha	Author of the 6th-7th century CE epic poem *Sisupālavadha*, much praised by later critics.
Manovinoda	A poet found only in some anthologies. Probably from late 12th century CE Bengal.
Murāri	Author of the play *Anargharāghava*, probably from 9th century CE Kashmir.
Nārāyaṇa	Compiler of the *Hitopadeśa* collection of fables and verses under the Pāla potentate Dhavala Chandra, probably in the 10th century CE.
Nayachandra Suri	Jaina monk, author of the *Hammīra Mahākāvya* on the life and death of the last Chauhan dynasty ruler of Ranthambor, who was defeated by Sultan Alauddin Khalji of Delhi in 1301 CE.
Nīlakaṇṭha Dīkshita	Prolific poet from 17th-18th century Madurai. His works include the epic *Śivalilārṇava* and the satire *Kaliviḍambana.*
Rājaśekhara	Critic, poet and dramatist of the 10th century CE, often quoted in anthologies. Author of the plays *Karpúramanjarí* and *Viddhasālabhanjikā*, and a work on poetics, *Kāvya Mīmāmsā.*
Ravigupta	Buddhist philosopher of c. 8th century CE, quoted in various anthologies.

Rupa Gosvāmin	Follower of the 16th century saint Chaitanya Mahaprabhu of Bengal. Anthologist and author of *Ujjvalanīlamaṇi,* a work on poetics.
Śankara	The great Vedanta philosopher, usually dated to the 8th century CE. He is also credited with some well known devotional poetry.
Saraha	Buddhist siddha and teacher of c. 8th century CE, regarded as the author of the Apabhramśa *Dohākośa*, a collection of verses.
Sāvarṇi	A poet found only in some anthologies.
Siddha	Śvetambara Jaina monk from Srimāla in modern Gujarat. Author of the allegorical verse novel *Upamitibhavaprapancha Kathā* in 906 CE.
Śīlā Bhattarikā	Ninth century CE poetess known only through anthologies.
Somadeva	Eleventh century CE Kashmiri author of the *Kathāsaritsāgara*, the famous collection of stories in verse.
Subandhu	Author of *Vāsavadattā*, a c. 6th century CE prose romance with 13 introductory verses.
Śūdraka	Sātavāhana dynasty ruler of the 2nd-3rd century CE. His play *Mricchakaṭika* is well known in translation as *The Little Clay Cart.*
Śyāmilaka	Author of the satirical monologue *Pādatāḍitaka* (*The Kick*), probably from the 5th century CE.
Vallana	Pāla empire poet of the 9th century CE, also mentioned as Ballana.
Vālmīki	Known in tradition as the *ādi kavi* or 'first poet' and the author of the *Rāmāyana.* This epic poem is ascribed to the period 400-200BCE.
Vatsabhaṭṭi	Composer of the Mandasor inscription, 436 CE.
Vidyā	A Sanskrit poetess whose verses are available only in anthologies, Placed in the 8th century CE, and also known as Vijjā and Vidyakā.
Vikaṭanitambā	Ninth century CE poetess acclaimed by the celebrated later critic Rājaśekhara.
Viśākhadatta	Author of the 7th century CE political plays *Mudrārākshasa* and *Devichandragupta*, drawn

	respectively from the history of the Maurya and the Gupta dynasties.
Vishnu Śārmā	Reputed compiler of the *Panchatantra*, the celebrated collection of fables dated to the 4th century CE.
Vyāsa	The traditional author of the *Mahābhārata*. The kernel of this long epic poem is believed to have been composed in the 5th century BCE.
Yaśovarman	Identified with the 8th century CE ruler of Kannauj of the same name. Author of the play *Rāmabhyudaya*.
Yogeśvara	Pāla period poet, praised by Abhinanda.

The Translators

Arnold, Sir Edwin	Poet, journalist and scholar (1832-1904). His translations from the Sanskrit include those of the *Hitopadeśa* and the *Gitagovinda* and the *Song Celestial*, a verse rendering of the *Bhagavadgita*.
Aurobindo, Sri	Celebrated savant and Indian nationalist (1875-1950)
Basham, Arthur L.	Indologist (1914-1986). Was Reader in Indian History, University of London, and Professor of Asian Civilization, Australian National University. His major work is *The Wonder that was India* (1954).
Brough, John	Indologist (1917-1984). Was Professor of Sanskrit, University of Cambridge. Translated *Poems from the Sanskrit* (1968).
Brown, W. Norman	Indologist (1892-1975). Was Professor of Sanskrit, University of Pennsylvania.
Dent, Peter	British poet and translator.
Dutt, Romesh C.	Administrator and scholar (1845-1909). Indian Civil Service, 1871-1891. His verse translations from the *Ramayana* and the *Mahabharata* were first published in 1899. President, Indian National Congress, 1899.
Edgren, A. Hjalmar	Swedish Sanskritist. His translation of Kalidasa's Shakuntala appeared in 1894
Gerow, Edwin	Professor of Sanskrit, University of Chicago. His published works include *Indian Poetics* (1977).
Gitomer, David	Instructor in the Department of Middle East Languages and Cultures, Columbia University, New York.
Griffith, R.T.H.	Was Principal, Benaras College. Translated *Hymns of the Rig Veda* (1889), and of the *Sama Veda* (1907).
Haksar, A.N.D.	Former Indian diplomat who has translated from the Sanskrit the, *Daśa Kumāra Charita* the *Simhāsana Dvātrimśikā* and the *Shuka Saptati* among others works.

Hume, Robert E.	Was Professor of the History of Religion, Union Theological Seminary, New York. Translator of *The Thirteen Principal Upanishads* (1921).
Ingalls, Daniel H. H.	Was Wales Professor of Sanskrit, Harvard University. His works include a translation of the *Subhāshita Ratnakosha* of Vidyakara (1965).
Isherwood, Christopher	Novelist, playwright and poet (1904-1986).
Johnston, E.H.	British scholar of Buddhism, best remembered for his translation of the *Buddhacharita* of Aśvaghosha (1936).
Jones, Sir William	Linguist, jurist and polymath (1745-1794). Founded the Asiatic Society in Calcutta, 1784. First translator from Sanskrit of *Śakuntalā* (1789), *Gita Govinda* (1792) and *Manusmriti* (1794).
Keyt, George	Noted Sri Lankan artist and poet.
Lal, P.	Poet and teacher, whose Writers Workshop has stimulated Indian creative writing in English. Transcreator of *Sanskrit Love Lyrics* (1966) and other works.
Le Mée, Jean	Born in France, 1931. Studied Sanskrit at Columbia University, and taught at the Cooper Union for the Advancement of Science and Art, New York. Translated *Hymns from the Rig Veda* (1975).
Masson, J. Moussaieff	Was Professor of Sanskrit, University of Toronto. Translator, with W.S. Merwin, of *Sanskrit Love Poetry* (1977).
Mathers, E. Powys	Distinguished translator of Sanskrit, Arabic, Chinese and Japanese verse.
Mehrotra Arvind Krishna	Indian poet, whose works include *Nine Enclosures* (1975), *Middle Earth* (1984) and *The Absent Traveller* (1991).
Merwin, W.S.	American poet, playwright, translator and Pulitzer Prize winner.
Miller, Barbara Stoler	Was Professor of Oriental Studies at Barnard College, Columbia University. Her translations include the *Gitagovinda* of Jayadeva (1979) and *The Hermit and the Love Thief* (1978).
Misra, Vidya Niwas	Taught Sanskrit and Linguistics at universities in Agra, Gorakhpur, Berkeley and Seattle. Noted writer

	on Indian culture and philosophy, and former Chief Editor, Navbharat Times. Vice Chancellor, Dr. Sampurnanada University, Varanasi.
Nandy, Pritish	Poet, editor and member of the Rajya Sabha.
Nathan, Leonard	American poet, Professor of Rhetorics at the University of California, Berkeley.
Pandit, Ranjit Sitaram	Indian scholar (d. 1944) whose translations include the *Ritusamhāra* of Kalidasa and Kalhana's *Rājataringini.*
Paz, Octavio	Mexican poet, scholar and diplomat (1914-1995). Winner of the Nobel Prize for Literature, 1990.
Pollock, Sheldon	George V. Bobrinskoy Professor of Sanskrit and Indic Studies, University of Chicago. His books include *Aspects of Versification in Sanskrit Lyric Poetry* (1977).
Prabhavananda, Swami	Monk of the Ramakrishna Mission who worked long years in California and translated several Sanskrit texts.
Raghavan, V.	Was Professor of Sanskrit, University of Madras, and an eminent Sanskritist.
Rajan, Chandra	Taught English Literature at Lady Shri Ram College, Delhi University and at the University of Western Ontario, Canada. Her translations include the *Complete Works of Kalidasa, volume I,* and the *Panchatantra.*
Ramanujan, A.K.	Poet, scholar and translator, chiefly of classical Tamil and Kannada poetry (1929-1993). Author of *The Interior Landscapes* (1967).
Ryder, Arthur W.	American Sanskritist (1877-1938). His translations include *Shakuntala and other writings of Kalidasa* (1912) and *Panchatantra* (1925)
Swami, Shree Purohit	Indian scholar who collaborated with W.B. Yeats in translating *The Ten Principal Upanishads* (1937).
Vatsyayan, Sacchidanand	Distinguished Hindi poet, novelist and critic (1911-1987).
Vivekananda, Swami	Famous saint, scholar and Indian nationalist (1863-1902).

Warder, Anthony K.	Professor Emeritus of Sanskrit, University of Toronto. Author of the multi-volume *Indian Kāvya Literature*.
Williams. Sir M. Monier	Indologist (1918-1899). Was Boden Professor of Sanskrit, Oxford University. His Sanskrit-English Dictionary (1899) is still current.
Yeats, William Butler	Irish poet (1865-1939). Winner of the Nobel Prize for Literature, 1923.

Endnotes

Introduction

1. A.B. Keith, A History of Sanskrit Literature, Oxford University Press, London, 1941.
2. Sri Aurobindo, The Secret of the Veda, Sri Aurobindo Birth Centenary Library, Pondicherry, 1972
3. A.W. Ryder, Kalidasa: Shakuntala and Other Writings, Dutton & Co, New York, 1912
4. Octavio Paz, In Light of Asia, The Harville Press, London, 1997, tr. Eliot Weinberger, 1997
5. A.L. Basham, The Wonder that was India, Random House, New York, 1954
6. Lin Yutang, The Wisdom of India, Random House, New York, 1942
7. Quoted in Barbara Stoler Miller, The Plays of Kalidasa: Theatre of Memory, Columbia University Press, New York, 1984
8. *Subhāshita Ratnakosha* of Vidyākara. Translated by D.H.H. Ingalls as An Anthology of Sanskrit Court Poetry, Harvard Oriental Series, Vol. 44
9. *Gāthā Sattasai* (*Gāthāsaptaśati*) of Hāla, c. 1st-2nd century CE; *Subhāshita Ratnakosha* of Vidyākara, c. 11th century CE, Bengal; *Saduktikarnāmrita* of Sridharadāsa, c. 1205 CE, Bengal; *Paddhati* of Sárngadhara, c. 1363 CE, Rajasthan; *Subhāshitāvali* of Vallabha Deva, c. 15th century CE, Kashmir.

Verse Excerpts

7. Indra is a prominent Vedic god, often identified with thunder and the onset of rain. In one legend he slays the cloud-dragon Vritra to release the waters. Tvashtri, another Vedic deity, is associated with building and construction. Dasa and Pani refer probably to groups of demons.

10. Split nuts of the vibhītaka tree were used as dice for gambling. Here they are called 'the brown ones'. The tree has been identified as *Terminalia Bellerica.*

12. Soma was the potent juice of an as yet unidentified plant, used in Vedic rituals.

22. In a game of dice with his cousin and adversary, the Kuru prince Duryodhan, the Pandava king Yudhishthir staked and lost his brothers, himself and finally his queen Draupadi, who was then summoned to the Kaurava assembly. Duhsasan is the brother and Karna the friend of Duryodhan. Bhima and Arjun are Yudhishthir's brothers. Bhishma, Drona and Vidura are Kuru elders.

24. Abhimanyu, the young son of the Pandava prince Arjun and his wife Subhadra, was surrounded and slain during the Mahabharata war. Salya, Sakuni and Jayadratha were among the warriors opposing him along with Duhsasan, cf. 22.

25. Pritha, better known as Kunti, was the mother of the Pandava princes, cf. 22. Unknown to them, their enemy, the Kuru warrior Karna, was also her son born of the sun god Surya.

26. The mother is the queen Vidura exhorting her son, disheartened by defeat, to fight again. The account is related by Kunti to Arjun.

28. Savitri, the wife of Satyavan, was with him when he was overtaken by death while gathering wood in the forest.

34. As recounted in 31 to 33, Rama considered it his duty to go into exile and leave the kingdom of Ayodhya to his brother Bharat in fulfillment of a pledge made by his father. His wife Sita, and another brother Lakshman, insisted on going with him. Unsuccessful in persuading him to relent, Bharat begged Rama for his sandals, so that the kingdom may be governed in his name till he returned.

37. During their forest exile, Sita was abducted by the Rakshas king Ravana and taken to his island kingdom of Lanka. Rama's devoted friend, the ape Hanuman, located her there in a grove of Aśoka trees.

40. Yaśodhara is the wife of the Sakya prince Siddhartha. Chandaka is the loyal charioteer who drove him to the forest when he renounced the world.

42. Māra is the Tempter and embodiment of Desire who tried in vain to distract Siddhartha from his penance and meditation which led eventually to his Enlightenment, described in 43.

58. Living in exile, the Yaksha, a kind of demigod, asks a cloud to go to his celestial home and deliver to his beloved wife a message given in 59.

60. The marriage of the goddess Uma with the great god Śiva is described in this epic poem.

65. King Dushyanta recalls his meeting with the hermit maid Shakuntala, when they fell in love.

66. Pururava searches in the forest for his beloved wife, the nymph Urvasi, who has disappeared.

81. Valmiki and Vyasa are celebrated as the authors respectively of the epics *Ramayana* and *Mahabharata*.

94. Draupadi was a Pānchāla princess. She was humiliated by Duhsasan, as recounted in 23. Bhima, who swore vengeance at the time, captured the Kaurava prince during the Mahabharata war.

110. Rahu is a legendary planet which causes eclipses of the sun and the moon.

117. The sons of Daśaratha are Rama and Lakshman. They marched on Lanka to rescue Sita, earlier abducted by Ravana, the king of Lanka, as mentioned in 37. Ravana has twenty arms, equally adept in the martial and the fine arts.

118. cf. 81.

130. cf. 37.

140. The god of love traditionally wields five floral arrows to smite the heart.

158. Hari and Keshava are other names of the divine cowherd Krishna, also described in 156 and 157.

165. cf. 158. The cowherd is Krishna.